SAMPLER & ANTIQUE NEEDLEWORK ™

A Year in Stitches

Symbol of Excellence Publishers, Inc.

Sampler & Antique Needlework: A Year in Stitches

Copyright 1994 by Symbol of Excellence Publishers, Inc.
405 Riverhills Business Park
Birmingham, AL 35242
USA

Published by Symbol of Excellence Publishers, Inc.

ISBN: 0-932437-02-8
Manufactured in the United States of America

Publisher: Phyllis Hoffman

Executive Editor: Barbara Cockerham

Editor: Diane Kennedy-Jackson

Copy Editor: Lorna Reeves

Editorial Assistants: Susan Branch, Carol Odom

Production Vice President: Wayne Hoffman

Production Director: Perry James

Creative Director: Mac Jamieson

Executive Art Director: Yukie McLean

Art Director: Michael Whisenant

Graphic Designers: Dottie Barton, Scott Begley, Rick Nance

Photography Stylist: Cathy Muir

INTRODUCTION

Needlework possesses a rich and fascinating past that predates recorded history. From records that do exist, we can surmise that from very early times, needleworkers used the crudest of materials and tools to create utilitarian pieces that are today considered to be works of needle art. Within the realm of needlework lies samplermaking. While the earliest surviving example of what is believed to be a sampler from the early Nazca culture dates to between A.D. 200 and 500, samplermaking's recognized history dates from approximately the sixteenth century forward.

The making of samplers in times past provided a means by which a young lady learned the alphabet and numerals. But much more importantly, it taught her the needle skills she was required to master in order to be considered suitable for marriage. One of her primary responsibilities was to mend, tend, and mark the linens and clothing needed for a household.

Sampler stitchers of modern times enjoy samplermaking as a pleasurable hobby. While many of us ply the stitches to re-create masterworks from the past, we also have an incredible array of contemporary work from which to choose. The appeal for some may be simply to create beautiful, decorative pieces for their homes. For others, however, their pastime also serves to educate them to the art of the needle while stimulating interest in its origins. For those individuals, existing samplers from days gone by offer not only a glimpse at the techniques that were used to execute them but also a look at the times in which they were created. They speak to the morals and values of their times, as well as to the political and educational influences that affected entire cultures. They are a mirror of a way of life that has long since passed.

It is the continued pursuit of education and joy in the needle that brings us together as stitchers to marvel at the skills of needle artists from the past, to educate ourselves to the skills and the history of the needle, and to leave a samplermaking legacy for future generations.

CONTENTS

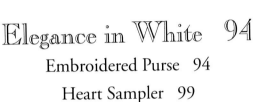

Frances Lawson Sampler

The antique Frances Lawson Sampler, dated 1836, is indicative of a young child's work, as evidenced by Frances' tender age of seven, which is stitched on her sampler. The extensive amount of red fiber used in this piece makes it a bit unusual. Perhaps even more remarkable, however, is the minimal amount of fading that has occured through the years.

Comprised of wool and cotton fibers, this sampler, a reproduction of the antique *Frances Lawson Sampler*, is worked entirely in cross stitch over either one or two threads. Simple in its execution and charming in its design, this piece will be wonderful for the beginning samplermaker or for the more-experienced enthusiast who would welcome a respite from complex needleworking endeavors. The strawberry band dividing the verse from the remainder of the sampler is typical of eighteenth- and nineteenth-century strawberry border patterns. The baskets and trees were also commonly used on pieces from this period.

Let gratitude in acts of goodness flow;
Our love to God, in love to man below.
Be this our joy—to calm the troubled breast,
Support the weak, and succour the distrest;
Direct the wandrer, dry the widows tear,
The orphan guard, the sinking spirits cheer.
Tho' small our pow'r to act tho mean our skil
God sees the heart, he judges by the will.

Done by Frances Lawson aged 7 years 1836

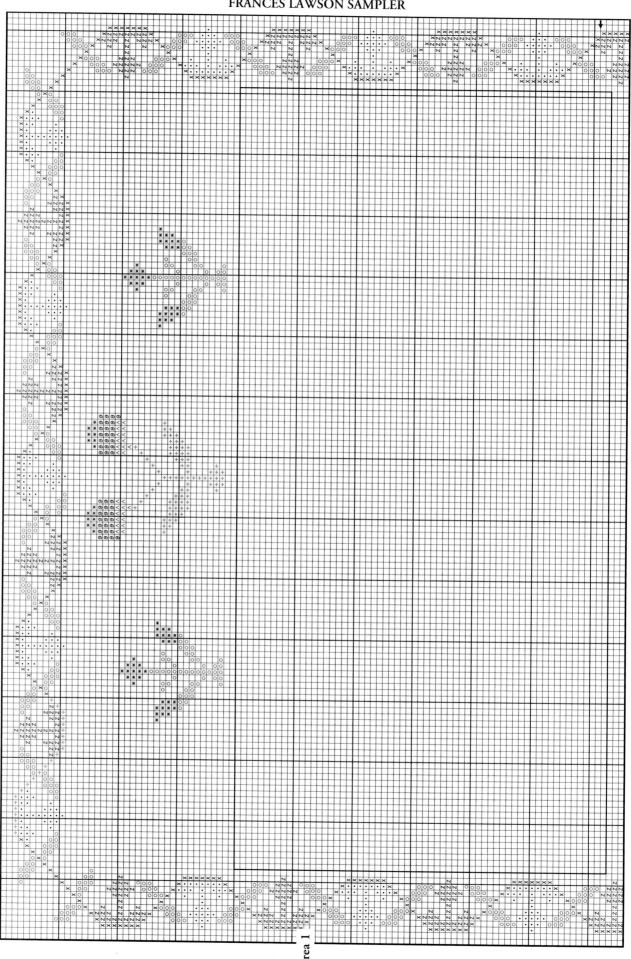

Area 1

Shaded portion indicates overlap from previous page.

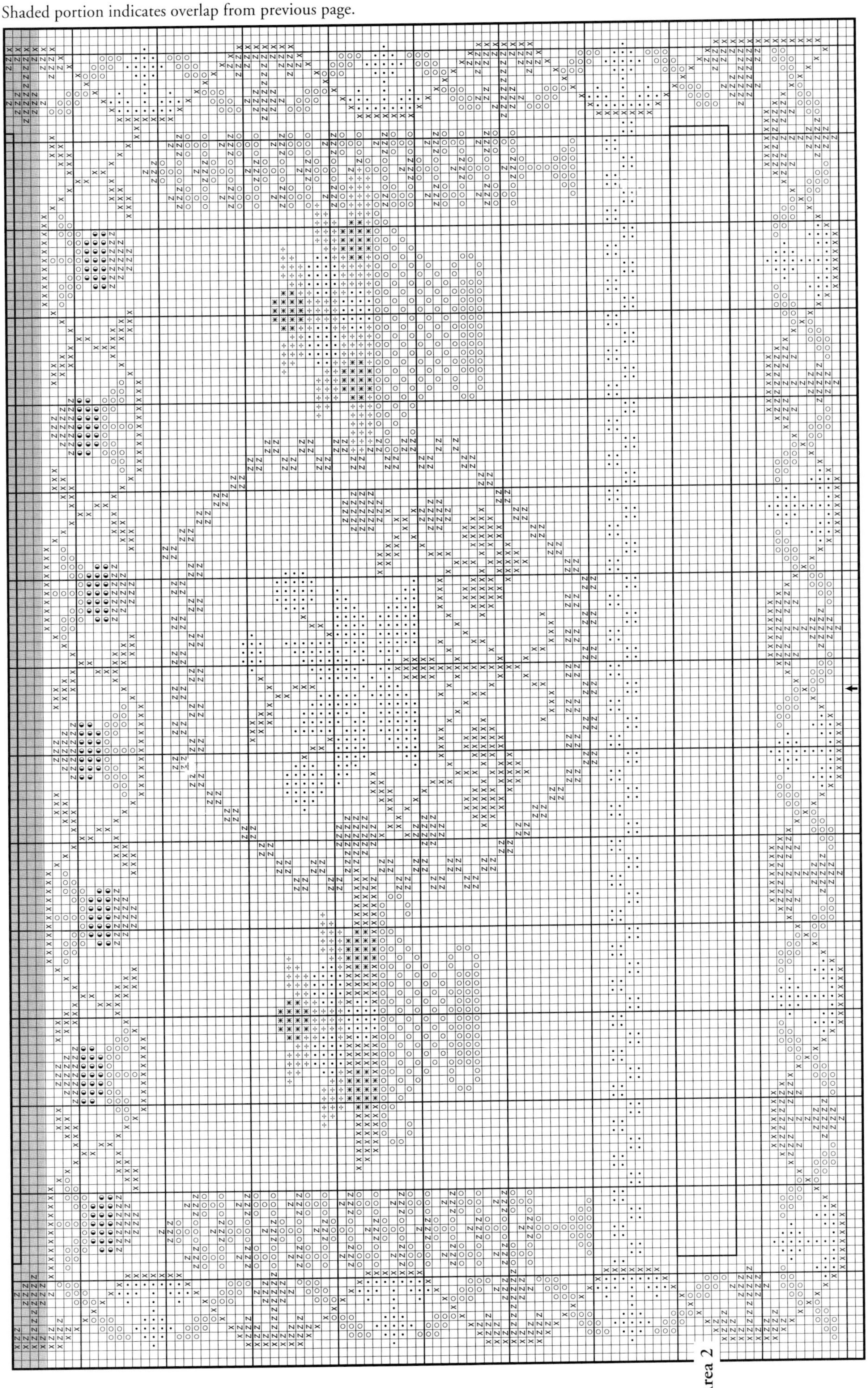

Area 2

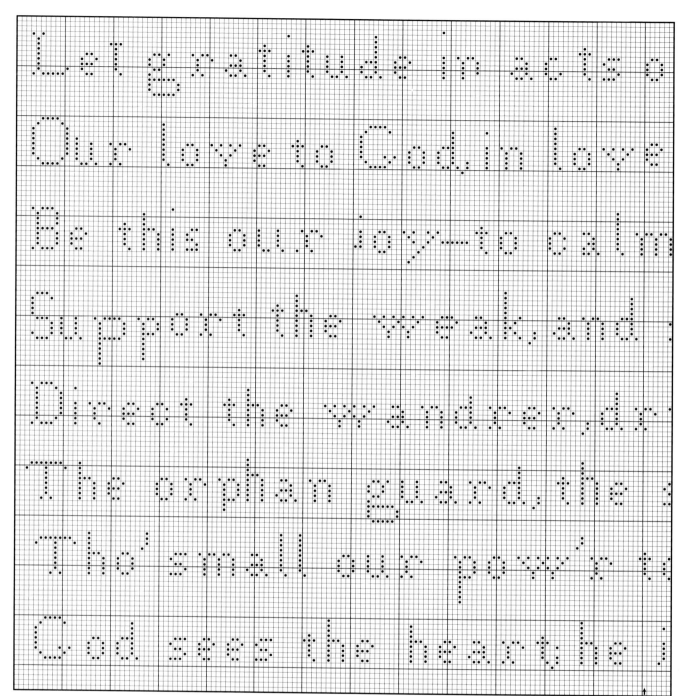

Area 1

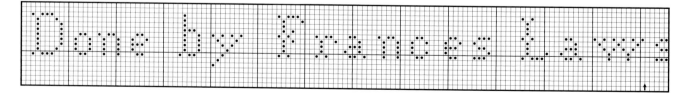

Frances Lawson Sampler

DMC		Kreinik	
Medicis	DMC	Soie d'Alger	
◑ 8100	815	946	garnet, med.
✳ 8126	347	2916	salmon, dk.
Z 8127	349	936	coral, dk.

𝟫 8223	760	2914	salmon
∧ 8313	729	2242	old gold, med.
• 8509	762	1732	pearl gray, vy. lt.
÷ 8422	3011	3724	khaki, dk.
X 8406	3363	1843	pine green, med. (two skeins)
○ 8400	833	2234	olive, lt.
● 8500	3371	4136	black-brown

Fabric: 28-count vintage linen from Wichelt Imports, Inc.
Stitch count: 198H x 149W
Design size:

25-count	15⅞" x 12"
28-count	14⅛" x 10⅝"
32-count	12⅜" x 9⅓"
36-count	11" x 8¼"

Shaded portion indicates overlap from previous page.

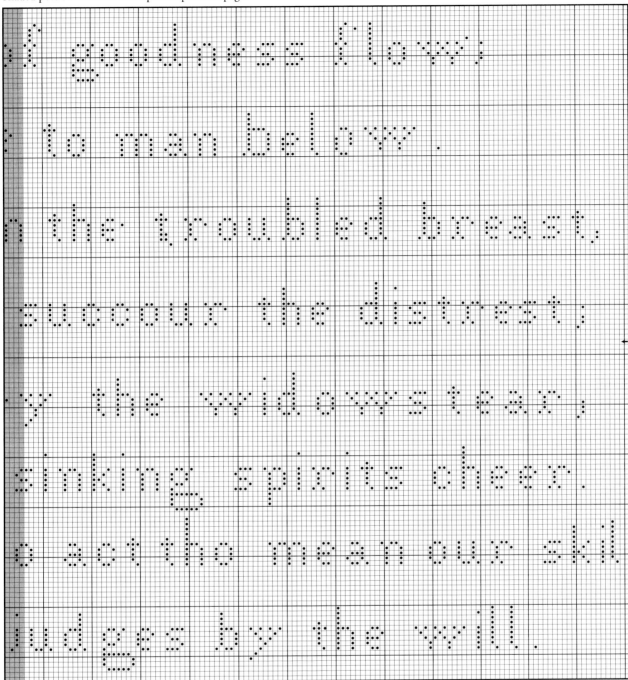

Shaded portion indicates overlap from previous page.

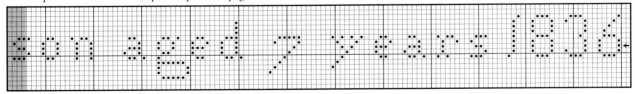

Area 2

Instructions: Cross stitch over two threads, using one strand of wool unless otherwise indicated.

Special instructions:

Areas 1 & 2: Cross stitch over one thread, using one strand DMC 3371.

Elizabeth Burcham Sampler

The Elizabeth Burcham
Sampler, dated 1806, is an
uncomplicated piece that is typical
of early works in the samplermaking
education of young ladies. Note that
the letter Y *in the lowercase, over-*
one alphabet is stitched backward.

This reproduction of the *Elizabeth Burcham Sampler* includes Algerian eye stitches and cross stitch over both one and two threads and was completed using a single floss color, as was the original. Containing a variety of alphabets and an assortment of dividing bands, as well as two sets of numerals, this simple piece is typical of a samplermaker's early work. Although Elizabeth's age is not included on her sampler, we can only guess from the simplicity of the design that she was fairly young when she completed her work.

Area 1

Area 2

Shaded portion indicates overlap from previous page.

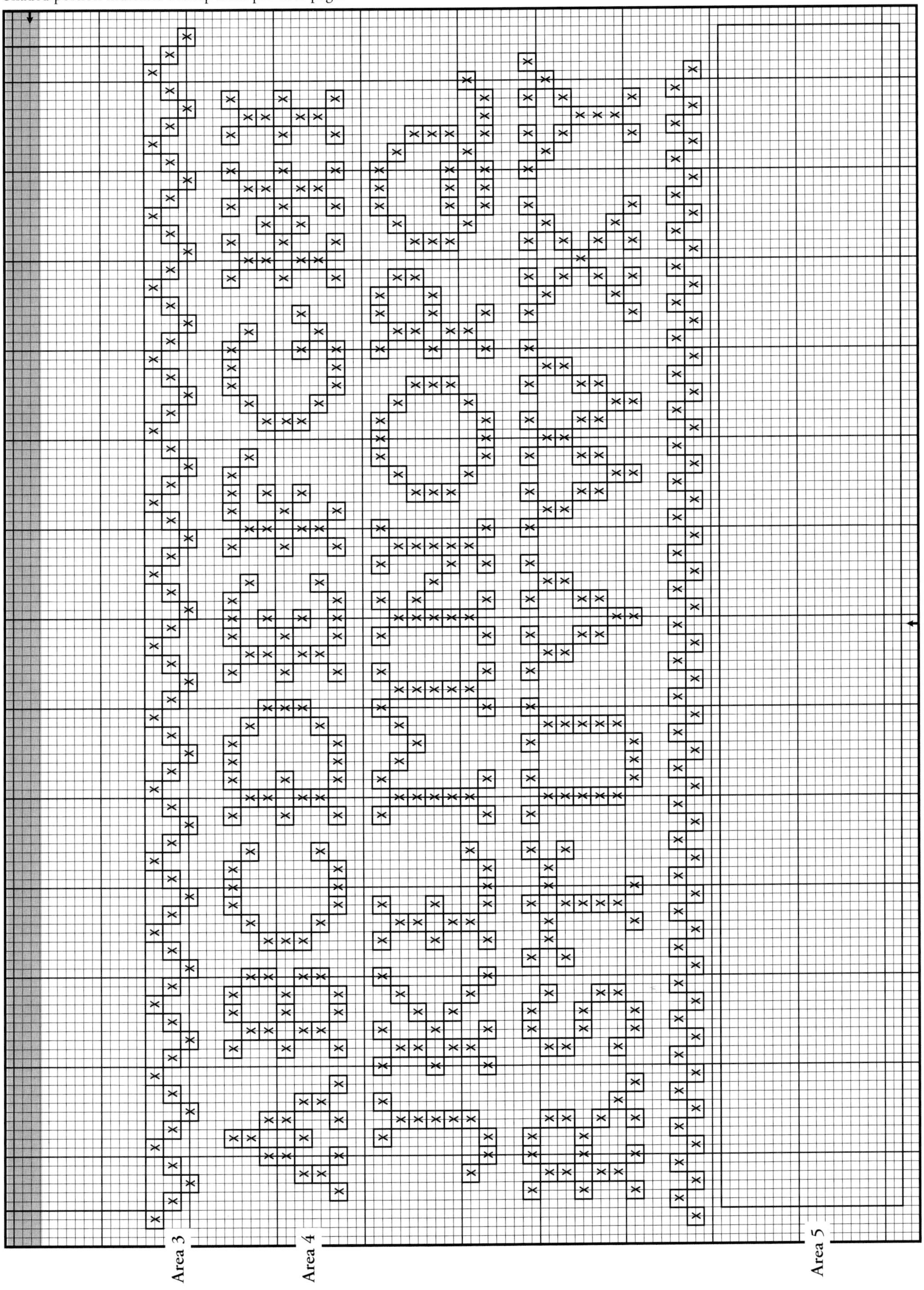

Area 3

Area 4

Area 5

17

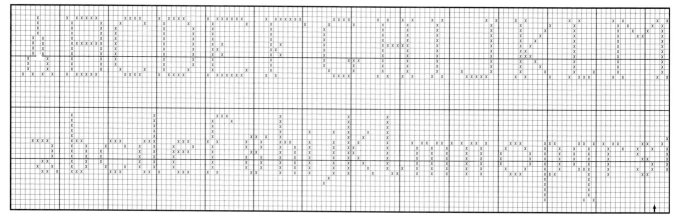

Area 2

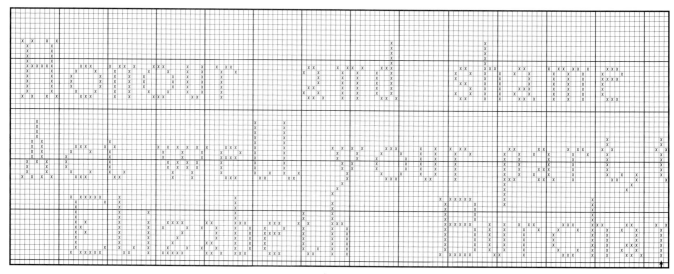

Area 5

Elizabeth Burcham Sampler

	DMC	Kreinik	
DMC	FT	Soie d'Alger	
X 924	2924	205	gray-green, vy. dk.
			(three skeins)

Fabric: 32-count ivory linen from Wichelt Imports, Inc.
Stitch count: 200H x 134W
Design size:
28-count 14¼" x 9½"
30-count 13⅜" x 9"

32-count 12½" x 8⅜"
36-count 11⅛" x 7½"

Instructions: Cross stitch over two threads, using two strands of floss unless otherwise indicated.

Special instructions:

Areas 1 & 4: Work Algerian eye stitch using two strands of floss.

Areas 2 & 5: Cross stitch over one thread, using one strand of floss.

NOTE: Large symbols indicate the placement of stitches worked over two threads.

Area 3: Work Algerian eye stitch using one strand of floss.

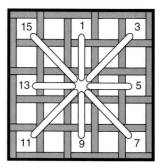

Algerian Eye Stitch

Shaded portion indicates overlap from previous page.

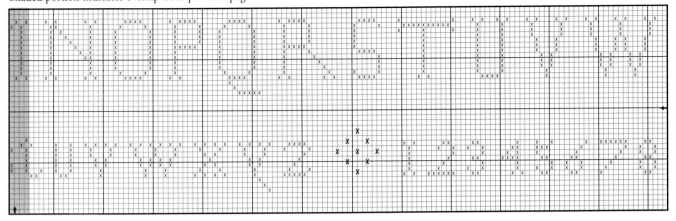

Shaded portion indicates overlap from previous page.

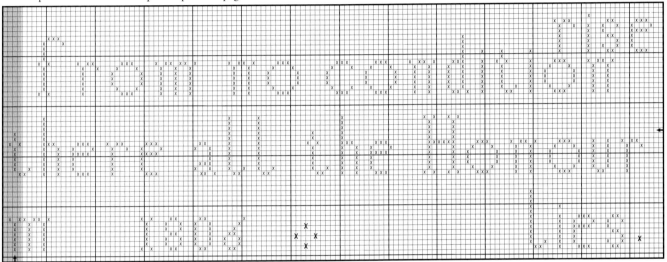

19

Dorothy Preston Sampler

This breathtaking, stitched masterpiece, a reproduction of the original *Dorothy Preston Sampler*, was worked on 40-count linen with an array of brightly colored silk floss. It contains a variety of stitches, including cross stitch, cross stitch over one thread, Algerian eye stitch, backstitch, upright cross stitch, and eyelet stitch worked over two threads. It was reproduced using silk-floss colors that are available today and that closely match the original colors, which are shown on the back of the antique piece. This beauty will grace the walls of any home in unforgettable style and will be a piece that any needleworking enthusiast will be proud to add to her collection.

Antique—Front

Antique—Back

*T*he antique Dorothy Preston Sampler, *an English sampler dated 1752, is in remarkable condition for its age. With only a few small holes in the ground fabric and several worn areas, this piece shows the artistry of the stitcher's work in magnificent detail. More damage has occured from light than perhaps any other element. The photograph of the back side of the piece shows the vividness of the original colors, while the photograph of the front shows evidence of the fading that has taken place.*

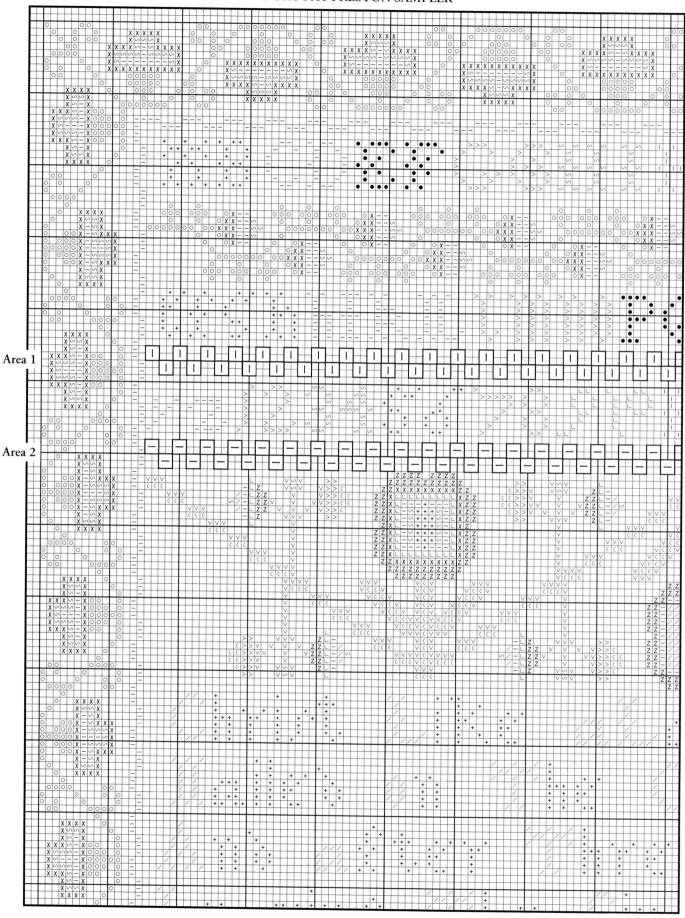

Area 1

Area 2

23

Area 3

Area 4

Shaded portion indicates **overlap** from previous page and page 23.

Area 5

Area 6

Shaded portion indicates overlap from previous page and page 24.

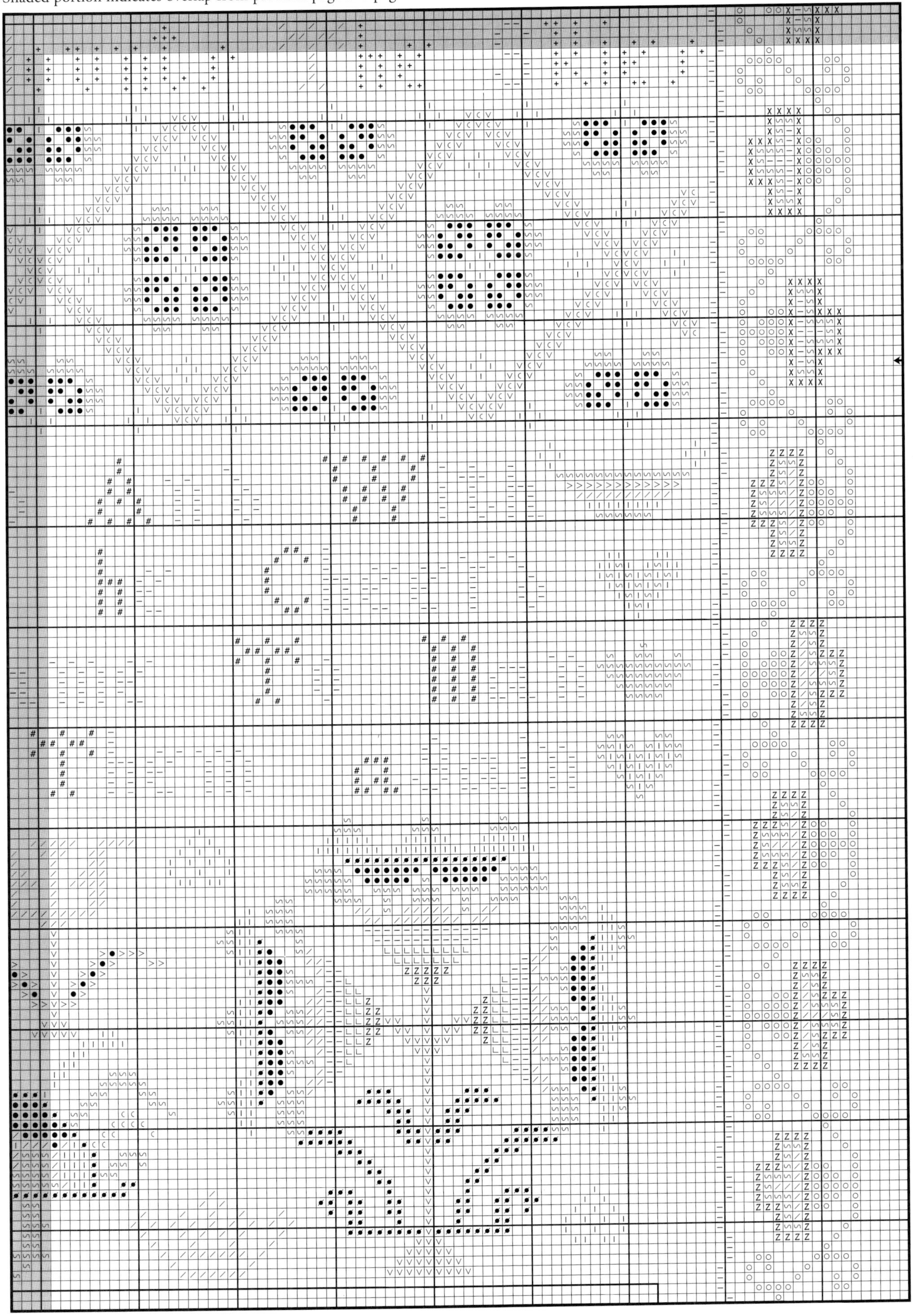

Area 7

Area 8

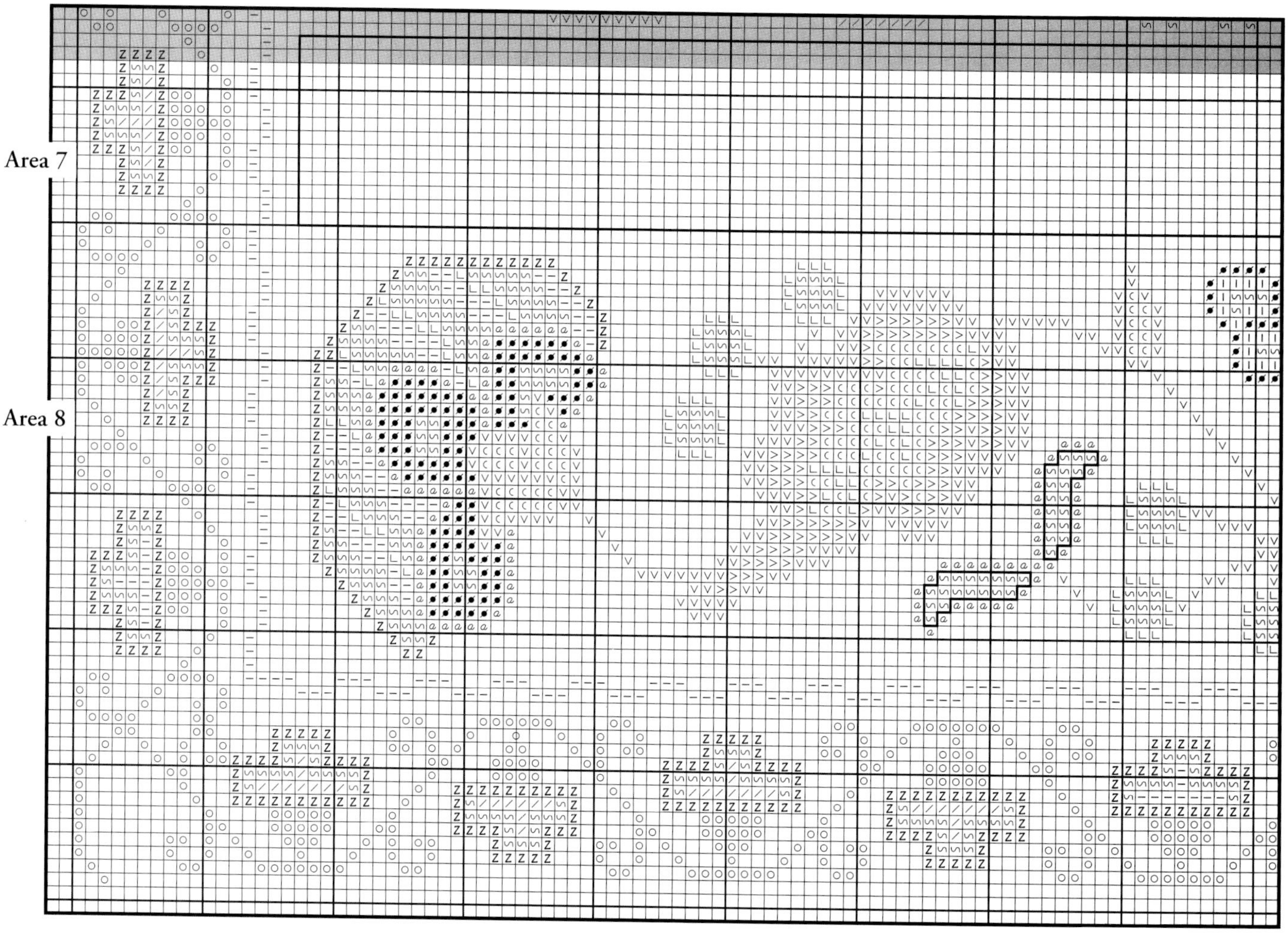

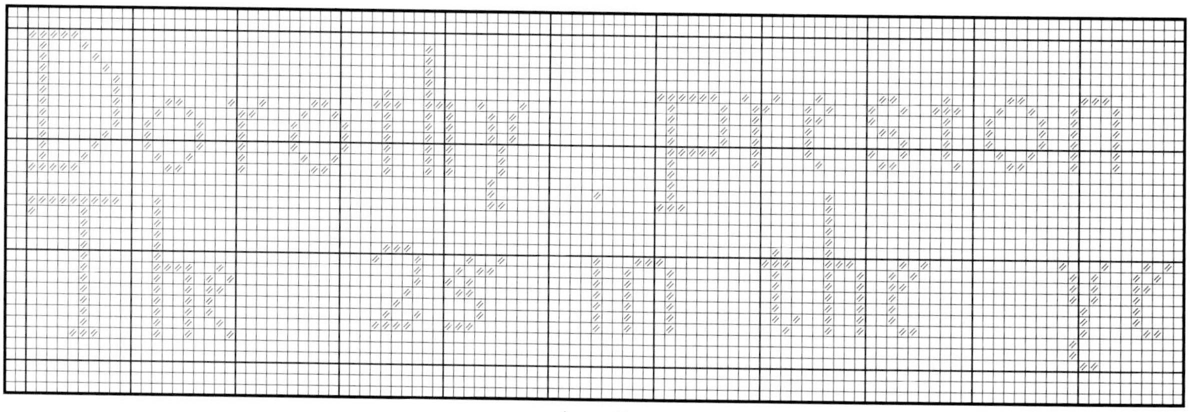

Area 7

Shaded portion indicates overlap from chart above, at right.

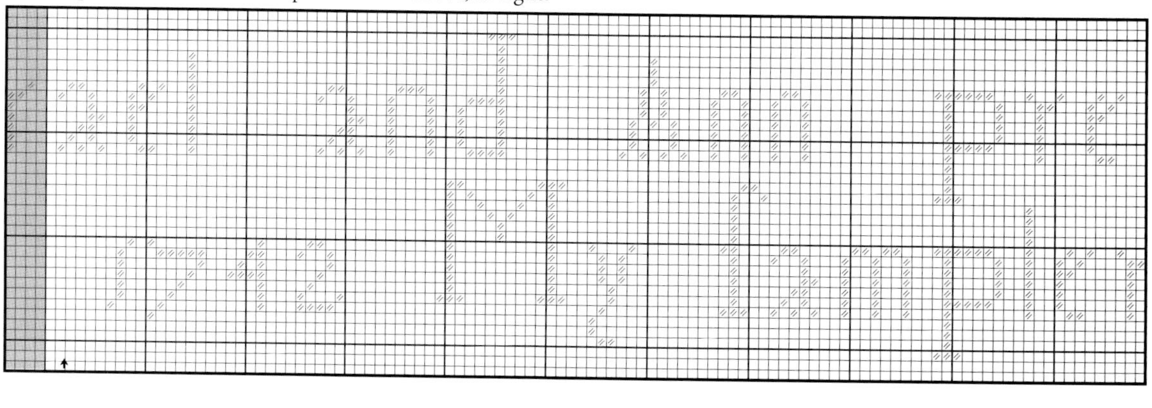

Shaded portion indicates overlap from previous page and page 26.

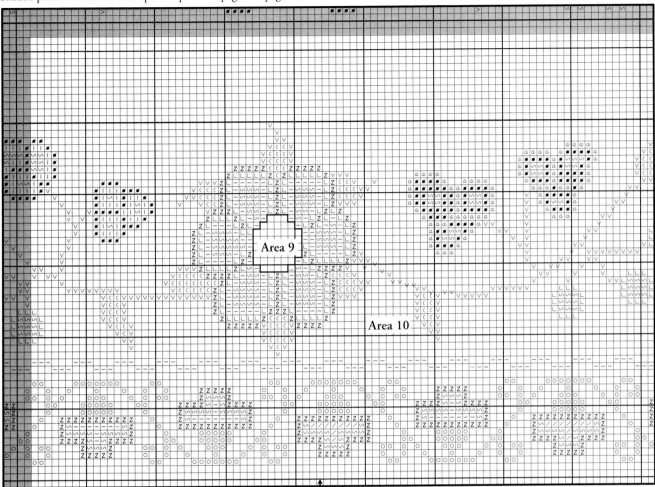

Shaded portion indicates overlap from previous page.

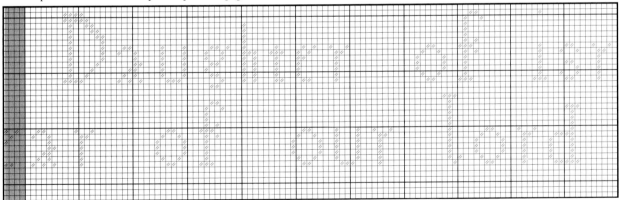

Shaded portion indicates overlap from previous page.

Shaded portion indicates overlap from previous page and page 27.

Area 7

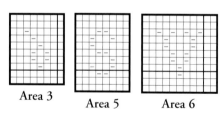

Area 3   Area 5   Area 6

Dorothy Preston Sampler

	Kreinik Soie d'Alger	DMC	DMC FT	
v	1844	890	2890	pistachio, ul. dk. (two skeins)
○	1835	3363	2469	pine green, med. (two skeins)
>	2125	469	2469	avocado
C	2145	581	2732	moss green
+	3423	524	—	fern green, vy. lt.
✒	1714	931	2931	antique blue, med.
ı	1743	318	2318	steel gray, lt.
∽	4531	3033	2613	mocha, vy. lt.
•	2513	727	2727	topaz, vy. lt.
–	946	816	2346	garnet (two skeins)
∕	3025	3350	2327	dusty rose, vy. dk.
L	4646	315	2315	mauve, dk.
Z	4612	356	2356	terra cotta, med.
∕∕	2626	3777	2354	terra cotta, vy. dk.
a	1425	823	2823	navy, dk.
X	4625	902	2902	garnet, vy. dk.
#	1715	3750	2929	antique blue, vy. dk.

Fabric: 40-count sandstone linen from Wichelt Imports, Inc.
Stitch count: 309H x 267W
Design size:

32-count	19¼" x 16¾"
36-count	17¼" x 14⅞"
40-count	15½" x 13⅜"
44-count	14" x 12"

Instructions: Cross stitch over two threads, using one strand of silk unless otherwise indicated. Backstitch using one strand of silk.

Special instructions:

Areas 1 & 2: Work Algerian eye stitch using one strand of silk.

Areas 3, 5, 6, & 7: Cross stitch over one thread, using one strand of silk.

Area 4: Work eyelet stitch over two threads for first letter of each word, using one strand of silk.

Area 8: Backstitch using one strand of silk.

Area 9: Work upright cross stitch over four threads, using one strand of floss and working compensating stitches over two threads as needed to fill in area.

Area 10: This area includes displaced cross stitch. When symbol is placed over a line, the stitch should be placed in that position and worked over two threads.

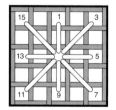

Algerian Eye Stitch

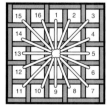

Eyelet Stitch

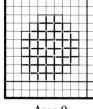

Area 9

Westtown Samplers—Quaker Heritage

Westtown School, from its position crowning the gently rolling hills on a six-hundred-acre, Chester-County site in eastern Pennsylvania, appears today much as it did almost two hundred years ago when the first students arrived by stagecoach or hay wagon. Walking on the quiet, peaceful campus, it is easy to imagine the school as it was in those early days, when the sons and daughters of Quakers from the surrounding area came to begin boarding and learning at the school.

Today, however, when a bell signals the end of the structured school day, the tranquility is broken as exuberant teens, dressed not in the plain garments of the Quakers, but in brightly colored shirts, jeans, and tennis shoes, with backpacks filled with books, leave the classrooms and make their way across campus. Opened in 1799 by the Religious Society of Friends in Philadelphia for the purpose of educating Quaker children, Westtown School remains the oldest boarding school in continual use in the United States.

More important, perhaps, to those concerned with American needlework history is the legacy of samplers left by the female students who inhabited these grounds in the early 1800s. Plain darning samplers, in keeping with the austere and practical approach to living embraced by the Friends, as they prefer to be called, were stitched in profusion by the young girls; and the dimensional globe samplers they worked are unlike any other samplers created in this country.

As the two-hundredth anniversary of the founding of Westtown School approaches, more than one hundred seventeen samplers and twelve globe samplers are housed in secure locations in the school's buildings. Most were stitched at the school and donated in recent years by descendants of the samplermakers; others were gifts and are similar in nature to the Westtown pieces. Five categories of samplers, which demonstrate a variety of stitching skills, were worked at the school: darning, alphabet, extract, geometric, and globe.

In a time when education for girls was rather limited at best, Quaker leaders provided the opportunity for girls to gain the same basic education that was offered to boys, with the addition of sewing and needlework. From the opening of the school until the mid-1800s, female students were required to spend two out of every six weeks stitching samplers. Since so much time was devoted to the study of stitchery, girls were excused from advanced mathematics and studied only elementary math.

The needlework requirement was dropped in 1843, according to Dr. Esther Pruett, Clerk of History and Antiques at Westtown School, because "the girls wanted to stitch things that were too fancy for Quakers. The matron was forever having to destroy fancy pincushions and that sort of thing, for they were not plain enough. The work was to be utilitarian, not at all fancy. The trustees felt the students were not adhering strongly enough to Quaker principles of quietness, piousness, silence, and non-decoration."

Dr. Pruett also serves as chairman of the bicentennial committee. She represents

The largest building, above, on the campus of Westtown School, houses the Upper School, administrative offices, the library, the dining room, and dorm rooms for boarding students.

Mary Garrett worked seven darning patterns on her tonal sampler, at left, stitched in 1816 at Westtown School. Like most darning samplers of the time, her piece is centered with a block created using chain stitch that resembles knitting. Note the spelling of the school name on the sampler.

the fifth generation of her family to receive an education at the school. When she attended Westtown for four years as a boarding student, she continued a family tradition begun by her great-grandfather.

"My grandmother met my grandfather because they were both waiting tables. (Students were required to help with tasks such as serving in the dining room or gardening.) There were separate dining rooms at the time for the boys and the girls, and my grandmother fussed until the day she died because the only time she could see my grandfather was when they met in the kitchen, bringing out dishes."

Beginning female students, often as young as age nine, were given plain sewing

*S*arah Mitchell Wilson worked her geometric half-patterns on dark-green linsey-woolsey and included the school name, spelled as Weston. Although she included only her initials, school records identify Sarah as the sampler's maker.

and darning to master as learning pieces. The goal of the teacher was to properly instruct the student so that she could take a rectangle of fabric, usually eight inches by twelve inches, and make darning repairs so perfectly that the mended areas could hardly be distinguished from the original fabric. The student would work five or seven blocks of darning patterns, each different, with the center block typically worked using chain stitch to simulate knitting. She would also include on her sampler her name, the date, and the school name.

The darning samplers that remain as a testimony to the needle skills of these students speak volumes not only about the students' ability with needle and thread but also about the philosophy of the Quakers themselves. Their emphasis on simple living is mirrored in the quaint charm of monochromatic darning samplers stitched by young hands as a reference for the day when the girl would be required to do the mending in her own household.

During the first half of the nineteenth century, darning samplers were also produced in European countries in a myriad of colors and darning

*T*abitha Rowland stitched her extract sampler while she was a student at Westtown School in 1803. Typical of the extract format, the work contains a pious verse, the school name, the stitcher's name, and the year, all within an oval-shaped, vine-and-leaf border. Tabitha spelled the school name as West-Town Boarding School.

patterns and often were further embellished with stitched flowers, decorative borders, and various motifs, such as crowns. The Quaker counterparts at Westtown School were somber in contrast, serving simply as patterns to be used when darning repairs were necessary.

When the student had mastered the darning sampler, she was permitted to move to another project. Alphabet, or marking samplers stitched in drab brown or black were considered an important next step; and the samplers often contained as many as seven stitchings of the letters with some use of eyelet stitch. Some more-imaginative students included the vowels and many examples of punctuation marks in their marking samplers. A distinctive, bold, block-type alphabet, often regarded as a "Quaker alphabet," was frequently included as one of the many alphabets.

Next in the progression of stitchery pieces was the extract sampler, also stitched in black or brown. A somewhat oval-shaped, vine-and-scattered-leaf border, thought to have originated at Westtown, was used with the name of the school stitched at the top, inside the border. A verse, or extract, was then stitched, followed by the student's name and the year. The students often used outline stitch and satin stitch in addition to cross stitch for executing these works. Although the extract samplers stitched by students while at Westtown School were rather plain, as befitted the Quaker lifestyle, many examples of further-embellished extracts remain, perhaps stitched by students after they had left the school.

The geometric and half-geometric sampler patterns usually associated with Westtown School were worked using cross stitch around the sampler borders. Most were worked on light-colored linen; however, some examples stitched on dark fabric exist.

The globe sampler remains as perhaps the most challenging of all needlework taught at the Quaker school. Among the collection of historic memorabilia held at Westtown School is a letter from a student to her parents regarding the unusual school assignment:

"I expect to have a good deal of trouble in making them, yet I hope they will recompense me for all my trouble, for they will certainly be a curiosity to you and of considerable use in instructing my brothers and sisters, and to strengthen my own memory, respecting the supposed shape of our earth, and the manner in which it moves (or is moved) on its axis, or the line drawn through it, round which it revolves every twenty-four hours."[1]

According to Dr. Pruett, the globe samplers were made only at Westtown School. "The project must have been assigned by the sewing school, but must have had something to do with geography. I have nothing but admiration for the girls who made these. I couldn't take those little melon-shaped pieces, stitch them together, stuff them with cotton, and expect them to be round. I don't know how they did it."

The globe samplers were worked on silk fabric, with countries marked by outline stitch in silk thread, and other markings made using ink. Couched, silk threads were also used to mark the longitude and latitude lines. The globes usually represented the earth. However, some examples, such as one housed in the Chester County Historical Society, West Chester, Pennsylvania, are celestial globes. The size of these impressive works was small, from four-and-one-half inches to six inches in diameter.

Throughout the forty-four-year period of samplermaking at Westtown School, the name of the school was recorded on samplers, using at least four spellings—Weston, West-Town, West Town, and Westtown. The spelling of the name was standardized in 1880 but not before one student received a letter from her mother that read, "Dearie, how does thee spell Westtown?" The letter rests in the collection of historic papers at the school.

Although Westtown School remains committed to the Quaker educational philosophy of cultivation of the intellect and spirit, social responsibility, and a sense of global awareness and involvement, the makeup of the student body differs from the school's early days. In 1799, everyone associated with the school was Quaker. All the students, most of whom were from the greater Philadelphia area, were from Quaker backgrounds; and all the teaching was done by Quaker teachers. Today, approximately twenty percent of the student body comes from Quaker backgrounds; about twenty percent of the students represents minorities; and seven percent of the students are from other countries.

This large, geometric motif sampler, though identified by the school and year, was not signed by the maker. The center emblem, marked with two birds and documenting information, is surrounded by a variety of floral motifs, thirty-eight sets of initials, and a geometric half-pattern border on three sides. Unlike the majority of Quaker samplers of this period, this striking sampler was created using more than one floss color.

In 1799, all the students at Westtown School were boarding students. Today, students at the Quaker school range from pre-kindergartners to senior-high students. Students in grades nine and ten can choose to board at the school; students in grades eleven and twelve are required to board. Students in grades pre-kindergarten through eighth and those in grades nine and ten who do not board are day students from the surrounding community. Westtown School is a college-prep school, and a bulletin board in the hallway of the main building is covered with notices showing where the present senior class members will enter college in the fall.

Westtown School is a part of the Philadelphia Yearly Meeting, which owns the school; and the trustees, with the exception of a few at-large members like Dr. Pruett, are members of PYM. The school is located on Westtown Road, in Westtown, Pennsylvania.

EDITOR'S NOTE

The author gratefully acknowledges the assistance and cooperation of Dr. Esther Pruett and John R. Batley, business manager, in arranging a tour of the Westtown School campus and archives and in permitting photography of samplers housed at the school. The photographs are used by permission of Westtown School, Westtown, Pennsylvania 19395.

ENDNOTES

[1]Helen G. Hole, *Westtown Through The Years 1799-1942*, (Westtown, Pennsylvania, Westtown Alumni Association, 1942), 56.

Sarah Woodward stitched the alphabet seven times on her marking sampler dated 1805. The first prominent alphabet is today regarded as a "Quaker alphabet," with the letters J and Q dropping below the line of the all-capital letter alphabet. Sarah included some punctuation marks on her sampler and worked the school name in one of the four spellings used at that time. The maple frame surrounding Sarah's sampler was made from 4-inch x 4-inch bed rails from old school beds once used at the Quaker school. The rails were milled into frame moulding by Palmer Sharpless, Westtown School class of 1940 and assembled by Edward Sharpless, class of 1936.

Frances Jewkes Sampler

A reproduction of the original, the *Frances Jewkes Sampler* is remarkably beautiful. Although it was created with little more than a dozen different floss hues and is comprised of only three stitches: cross stitch over both one and two threads, satin stitch, and Algerian eye stitch, its finished appearance hints at a much more complex piece. Symmetrically balanced but for the stitcher's name, age, and the date, this design contains a pious verse and an assortment of the flora- and fauna-inspired motifs that were commonly found on samplers of the past, including a variety of floral motifs, as well as birds, butterflies, and squirrels.

The antique Frances Jewkes Sampler, dated 1848, appears at first glance to contain simply green, gold, and brown-colored flosses. Upon closer inspection, however, one notices the inclusion of both dark and light blue fibers, as well as colorful touches of crimson that were used in two matching floral motifs. Note that the young Frances Jewkes capitalized all the letters of Jesus' name. Perhaps this was an effort to make His name stand out from the remainder of the verse.

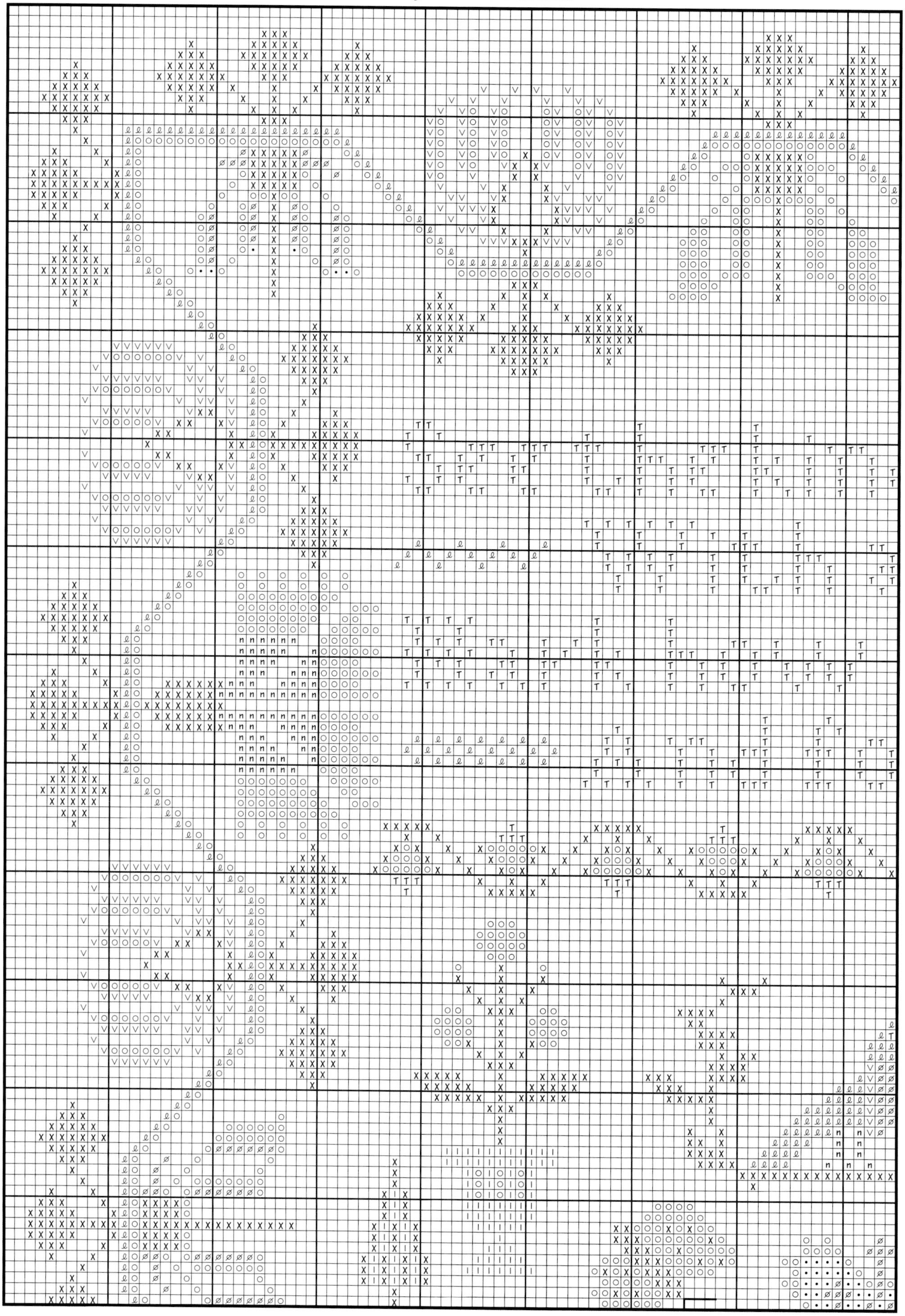

Shaded portion indicates overlap from previous page.

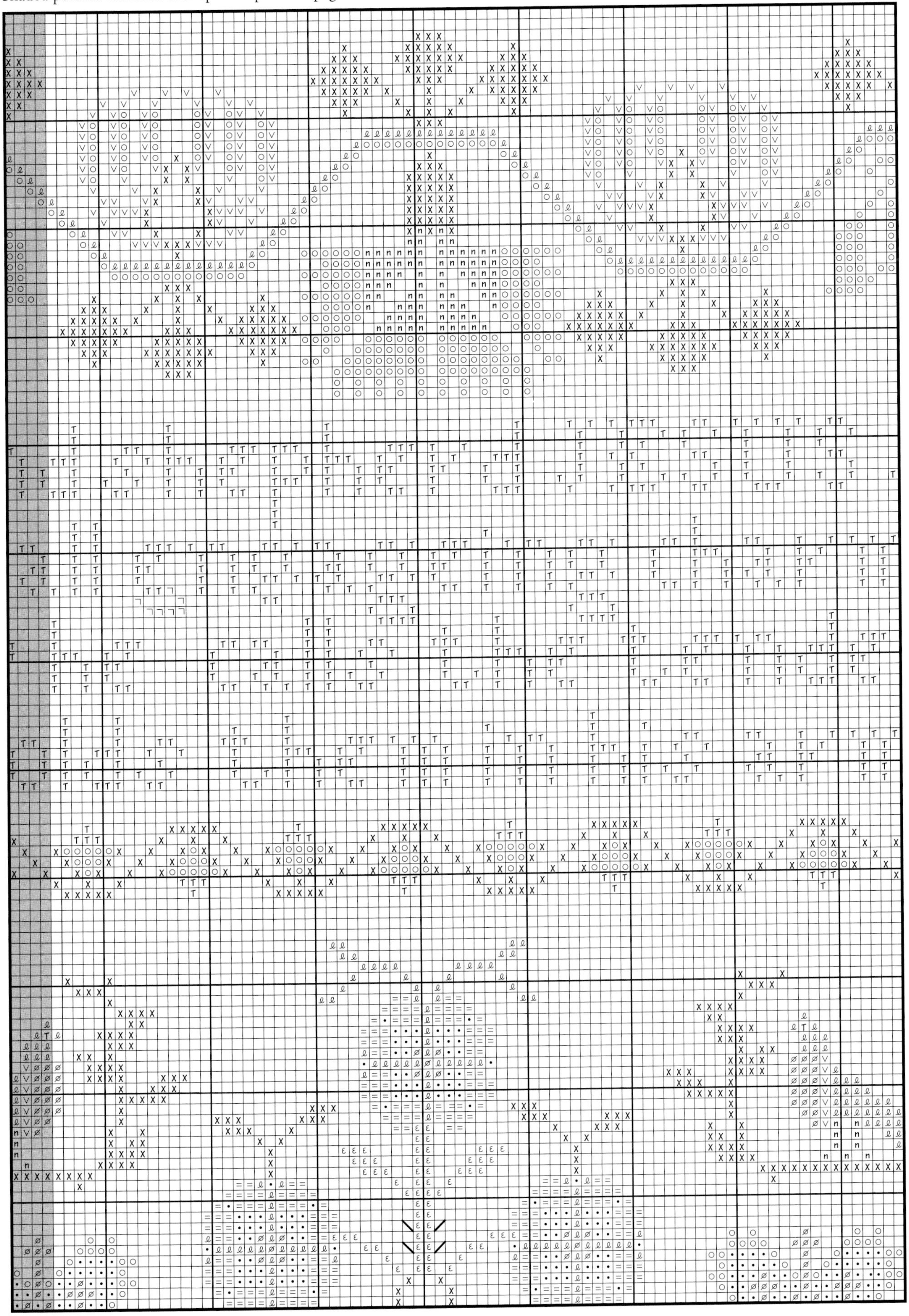

Shaded portion indicates overlap from previous page.

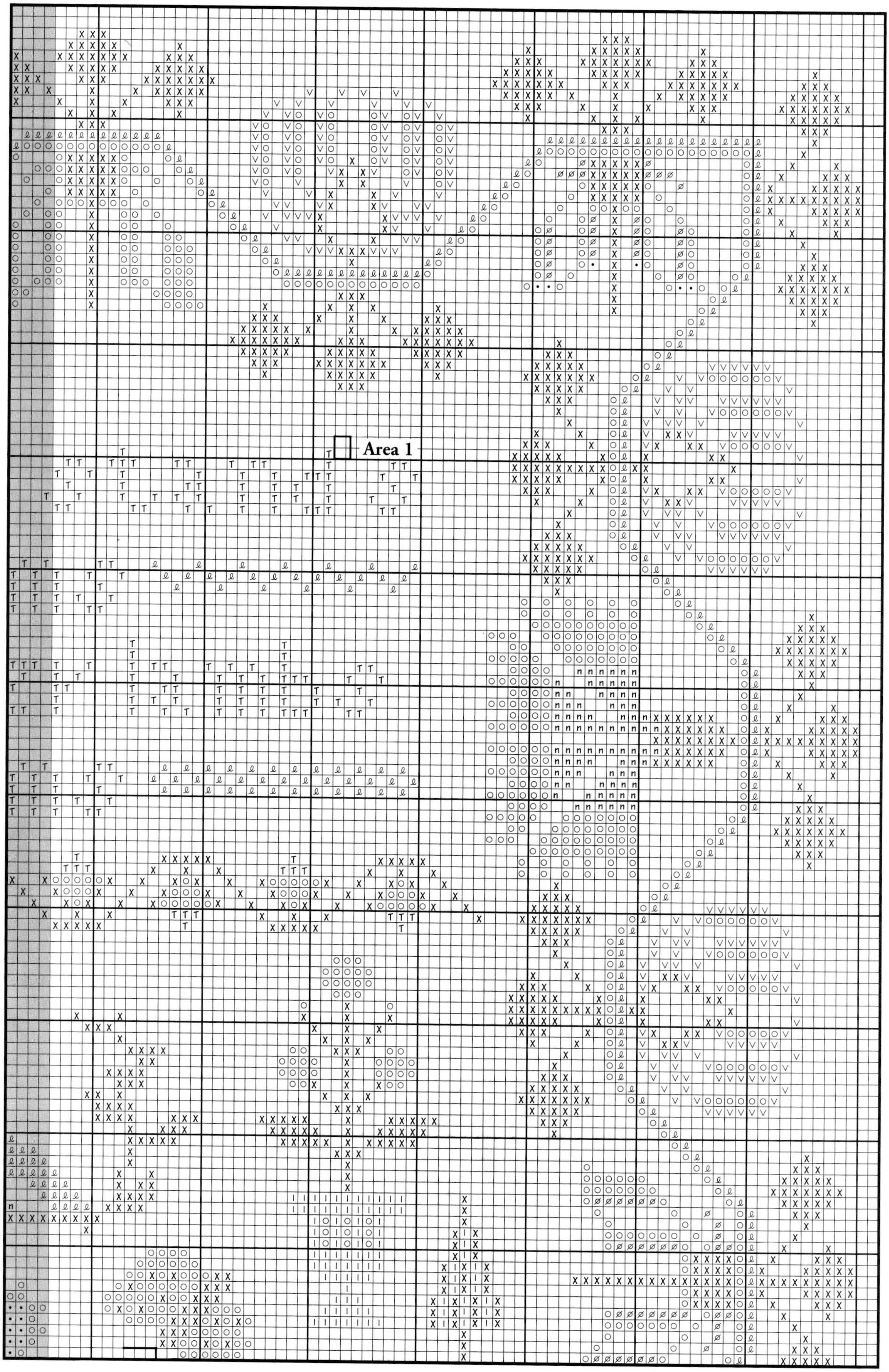

Shaded portion indicates overlap from page 36.

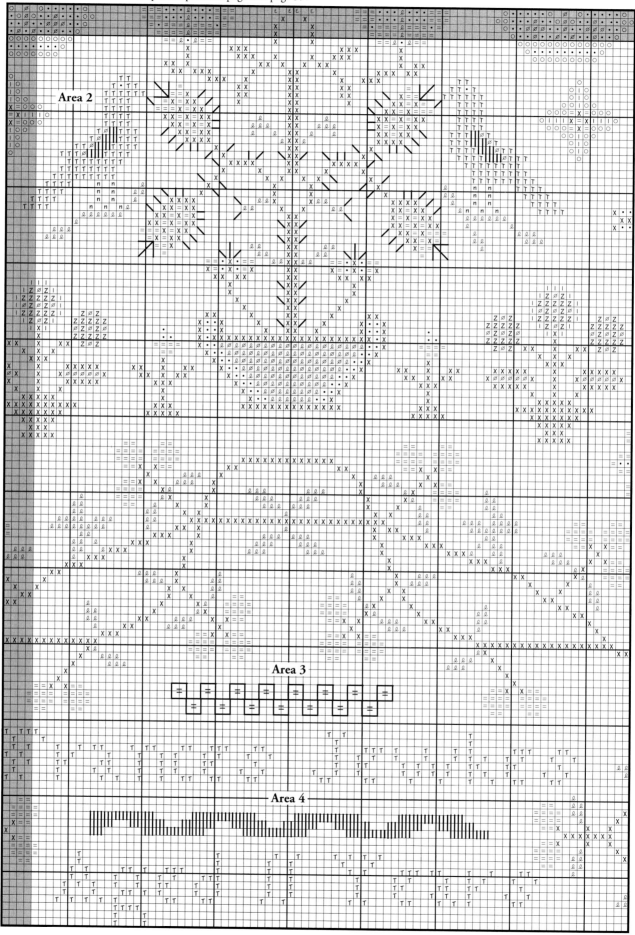

Shaded portion indicates overlap from previous page and page 38.

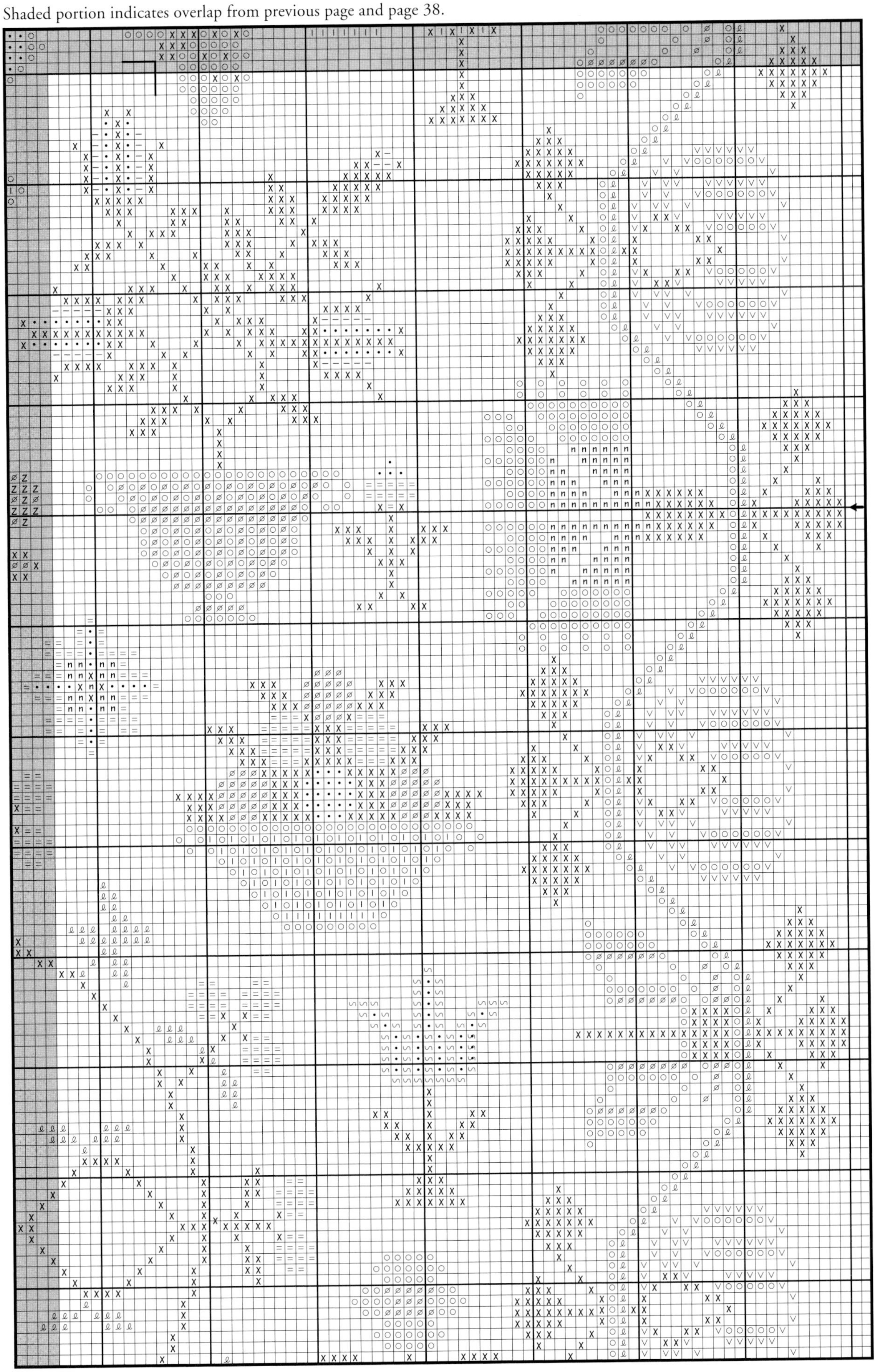

Shaded portion indicates overlap from page 39.

Frances Jewkes Sampler

Kreinik

	Soie d'Alger	DMC	DMC FT	
X	3426	500	2500	blue green, vy. dk.
ℓ	1843	503	2503	blue green, med.
ı	3422	524	—	fern green, vy. lt.
∽	1714	931	2931	antique blue, med.
Z	1424	311	2337	navy, med.

−	1026	326	2326	rose, vy. dp.
T	3836	3021	2371	brown-gray, dk.
L	3835	3787	2609	brown-gray, dk.
⌐	4536	611	2611	drab brown, dk.
•	brute	ecru	ecru	ecru
⌀	3831	822	2644	beige-gray, lt.
○	4532	613	2613	drab brown, lt.
v	3823	422	2673	hazelnut, lt.
=	4234	437	2738	tan, lt.
n	4243	680	2782	old gold, dk.

Fabric: 35-count cream linen from Norden Crafts
Stitch count: 316H x 238W
Design size:

25-count	25¼" x 19"
28-count	22½" x 17"
32-count	19¾" x 14⅞"
35-count	18" x 13⅝"

Instructions: Cross stitch over two threads, using one strand of silk. Work specialty stitches using one strand of silk.

Shaded portion indicates overlap from previous page and page 40.

NOTE: Where symbol Ɛ appears, cross stitch using 1843/503/2503 and then repeat using 3426/500/2500.

Straight-stitch instructions:

3836	3021	2371	birds' beaks
3426	500	2500	butterflies' antennae, thorns on buds of center motif
1843	503	2503	thorns on stalk of center motif

Special instructions:

Area 1: Cross stitch over one thread, using one strand of silk.

Area 2: Work satin stitch for birds' wings, using one strand 3831/822/2644.

Area 3: Work Algerian eye stitch using one strand of silk.

Area 4: Work satin stitch using one strand 4234/437/2738.

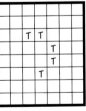

Area 1

43

Shaded portion indicates overlap from previous page and page 41.

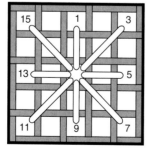

Algerian Eye Stitch

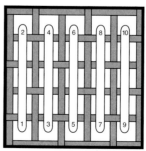

Satin Stitch

Eighteenth-Century Floral

Adapted from an eighteenth-century crewelwork design, this pillow top is reminiscent of the crewel embroidery of that period. Designed to include cross stitch as well as traditional crewelwork stitches, this piece is accented with colored beads. Finished as a pillow with complementary, shirred cording, this stitched treasure is also the perfect size to be used as a tray insert. Simply omit the beads so that the glass will remain flat or take the tray to a frame shop to have it fitted for spacers that will allow you to include the beads within the design beneath the glass.

The charming Eighteenth-Century Floral, an adaptation of a crewelwork design dated 1786, will be a stunning decorative piece wherever it is displayed.

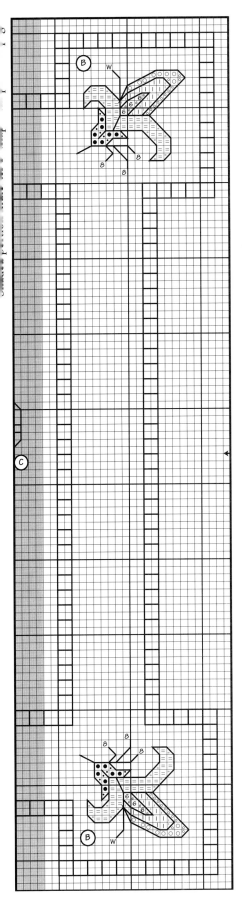

Eighteenth-Century Floral

DMC	Kreinik FT	Soie d'Alger	
╱ 676	2673	2243	old gold, lt.
6 729	2783	2242	old gold, med.
▮ 224	2223	4621	pink, lt.
○ 3722	2221	4623	pink, med.
✕ 221	2221	4624	pink, dk.
= 503	2503	122	blue green, med.
• 502	2502	1814	blue green
931	2931	1714	antique blue, med.
501	2501	3426	blue green, dk.
3750	2929	1716	antique blue, vy. dk.

Mill Hill Seed Beads

W   3003 red
8   3027 blue

Linen thread
    40/2 white

Fabric: 28-count antique white Glasgow linen from Zweigart®
Stitch count: 112H x 112W
Design size:

25-count	9" x 9"
28-count	8" x 8"
32-count	7" x 7"
36-count	6¼" x 6¼"

Instructions: Cross stitch over two threads, using two strands of floss. Backstitch using one strand of floss.

Backstitch instructions:

3722	2221	4623	tendrils of *Flowers A* and *C*
502	2502	1814	areas cross stitched in 503/2503/122
501	2501	3426	areas cross stitched in 502/2502/1814, stems other than main stems
729	2783	2242	areas cross stitched in 676/2673/2243, tendril of *Flower D*

Special instructions:

Flower A: Work center in block shading stitch, using two strands of floss. Work *Area 1* in outline stitch, using two strands 503/2503/122.

Flower B: Work center in outline stitch, using two strands of floss.

Flower C: Work scalloped sections in block shading stitch, using two strands of floss.

Flower D: Work in satin stitch, using two strands 676/2673/2243 for base of flower and two strands 729/2783/2242 for top of flower.

Flower E: Work in satin stitch, using two strands 931/2931/1714. Work buttonhole stitch around satin stitch, inverting stitch and using one strand 3750/2929/1716.

Leaf F: Work in outline stitch, using two strands of floss.

Main stems: Work in stem stitch, using two strands 501/2501/3426.

Borders: Work in four-sided stitch, using one strand linen thread.

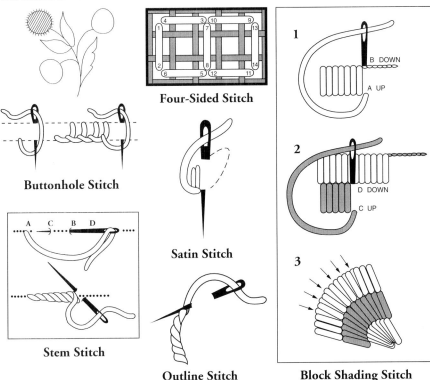

Four-Sided Stitch

Buttonhole Stitch

Satin Stitch

Stem Stitch

Outline Stitch

Block Shading Stitch

Rose Bouquet

The honor of wearing garments decorated with silk-ribbon embroidery once belonged only to royalty and wealthy members of eighteenth-century European courts. Ribbon embroidery has enjoyed periodic revivals in popularity since those long-ago years, in part, due to the development and distribution of new types of ribbons. "China ribbon," or narrow, woven-edge ribbon, appeared as early as 1842 but was used most extensively during the 1880s and 1890s; variegated French silk ribbon was introduced during the 1870s; and, today, the wide variety of Japanese silk ribbon that is available contributes to the renewed interest in silk-ribbon embroidery.

For the most part, silk-ribbon embroidery of the past was stitched upon garments, fashion accessories such as hats and parasols, and crazy quilts. The current trend still embraces clothing embellishment and stitching on accessories, such as brooches and handkerchiefs, but also includes silk-ribbon embroidery on household items, such as pillows, framed designs, box tops, and tea towels.

*T*he silk-ribbon Rose Bouquet Pillow and Box Top, *shown right and above, will carry you back to days of elegance as you stitch flowers, petals, and leaves with fine ribbon and your needle.*

Rose Bouquet

YLI Silk Ribbon

032	green, med.	(4mm)
157	mauve, lt.	(4mm)
158	mauve, med.	(4mm)
159	mauve, dk.	(4mm)
125	blue, lt.	(4mm)
081	blue, med.	(4mm)
156	ecru	(2mm)

DMC

white	white	
225	pink, vy. lt.	
501	blue green, dk.	
745	yellow, lt. pl.	

Mill Hill Seed Beads

2002   yellow creme

NOTE: Use of an embroidery hoop is recommended for these projects.

Spider-Web rose—Begin with five-spoke anchor stitch, using one strand DMC 225. Use all mauve-colored ribbons for each rose. Begin with darkest shade in center and work outward to the lightest shade. **NOTE:** Use tapestry needle to weave ribbon. For box lid, begin in center of rose with French knot.

French knot surrounded by lazy-daisy stitch—Work French knot using medium-mauve ribbon. Work lazy-daisy stitch using light-mauve ribbon.

Japanese ribbon stitch—Randomly work buds using all mauve-colored ribbons. **NOTE:** Do not pull too tightly or stitch will become a straight stitch. Work leaves and stem in fly stitch, using one strand DMC 501.

Japanese ribbon stitch—Work petals using light-blue ribbon. **NOTE:** Do not pull too tightly or stitch will become a straight stitch. Place one yellow seed bead in center of flower, using one strand DMC 745.

Straight stitch—Work leaves using medium-green ribbon.

Stem stitch—Work vine using two strands DMC 501.

French knot—Work bud using ecru ribbon. Work leaves and stem in fly stitch, using one strand DMC 501.

French knot—Work using two strands DMC white, wrapping floss around needle twice.

French knot. Work using medium-mauve ribbon.

Bow—Work using medium-blue ribbon, couching as indicated on pattern.

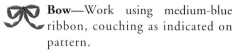

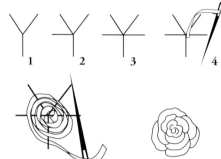

Spider-Web Rose

Straight Stitch

Japanese Ribbon Stitch

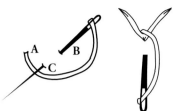

Fly Stitch

Trinket-Box Lid

French Knot

50

Stem Stitch

ROSE-BOUQUET PILLOW PATTERN

Needlework Casket

Containing a plethora of old sampler stitches, this incredible work of stitching art features five different designs: one for each panel of this beautiful, ladies' travel casket. The handcrafted, mahogany casket is a reproduction of a seventeenth-century piece found in the Victoria and Albert Museum in London. Included within the quintet of designs are some of the designer's favorite sampler motifs, as well as initials that trace the family lineage. Although this piece was created by the designer using motifs and initials to represent her family members, the enthusiast may use her own creativity to make it a personal treasure. Two young boys were stitched on the top panel, and additional charts have been included for girls. If working this panel to represent a larger family, the garden on the left-hand side may be omitted to accommodate additional figures. Sister stitchers on the front panel share the afternoon stitching and sipping tea. This panel will be a tribute to a cherished friendship when the initials of the needleworkers are included.

Needlework Casket

Kreinik

Soie d'Alger	DMC	DMC FT	
▲ 2126	935	—	avocado, dk.
– 1835	3363	2469	pine green, med.
• 3423	524	—	fern green, vy. lt.
∕ 3831	3033	2613	mocha, vy. lt.
■ 3344	3790	2609	beige-gray, ul. dk.
4 931	352	2352	coral, lt.
3 934	350	2350	coral, med.
⊠ 2916	347	2327	salmon, dk.
6 4232	543	2948	beige-brown, ul. lt.
v blanc	white	white	white
+ 1714	931	2931	antique blue, med.
\ 3336	550	2394	violet, vy. dk.
⋀ 3335	208	2532	lavender, vy. dk.
X 3026	3685	2814	mauve, dk.
○ 3024	3350	2327	dusty rose, vy. dk.
Z 2932	760	2760	salmon
✳ 2934	309	2309	rose, dp.
∧ 4536	840	2840	beige-brown, med.
r 946	816	2346	garnet
= 3013	3731	2329	dusty rose, vy. dk.
♡ 3021	3354	2761	dusty rose, lt.
♭ 2946	326	2326	rose, vy. dp.
W 4113	422	2673	hazelnut, lt.
△ 1012	754	2754	peach flesh, lt.
♦ 161	939	2823	navy, vy. dk.
P 1715	930	2930	antique blue, dk.
♯ 4516	434	2434	brown, lt.
✕ 4233	437	2738	tan, lt.
C 1724	931	2931	antique blue, med.
> 1712	3752	2933	antique blue, vy. lt.
L 3842	415	2415	pearl gray
★ 2136	936	2937	avocado, vy. dk.
♪ 3424	522	—	fern green
A 3416	—	—	stone
∪ 1735	413	2413	pewter gray, dk.
B 2231	3046	2673	yellow-beige, med.
⬛ 1835	3363	2469	pine green, med.
⬭ 3423	524	—	fern green vy. lt.
⬮ 3831	3033	2613	mocha, vy. lt.
⬯ 3344	3790	2609	beige-gray, ul. dk.
⬛ 931	352	2352	coral, lt.
⬭ 934	350	2350	coral, med.
⬛ 2916	347	2327	salmon, dk.
⬛ 2126	935	—	avocado, dk.
3323	3042	—	antique violet, lt.

Kreinik Metallics
#5 Japan Thread

Fabric: 36-count cream Edinborough linen from Zweigart®

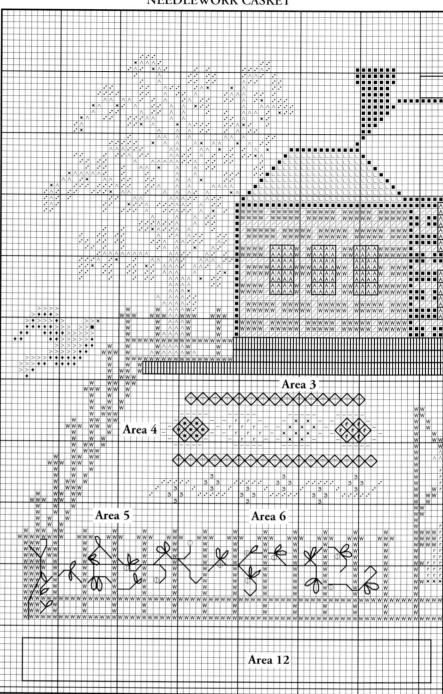

Area 3

Area 4

Area 5

Area 6

Area 12

TOP PANEL

Stitch count:

Top panel	107H x 176W
Grape & Strawberry panels	45H x 99W
Front & Back panels	45H x 171W

Design size:

Top panel	
36-count	6" x 9¾"
Grape & Strawberry panels	
36-count	2½" x 5½"
Front & Back panels	
36-count	2½" x 9½"

Shaded portion indicates overlap from previous page.

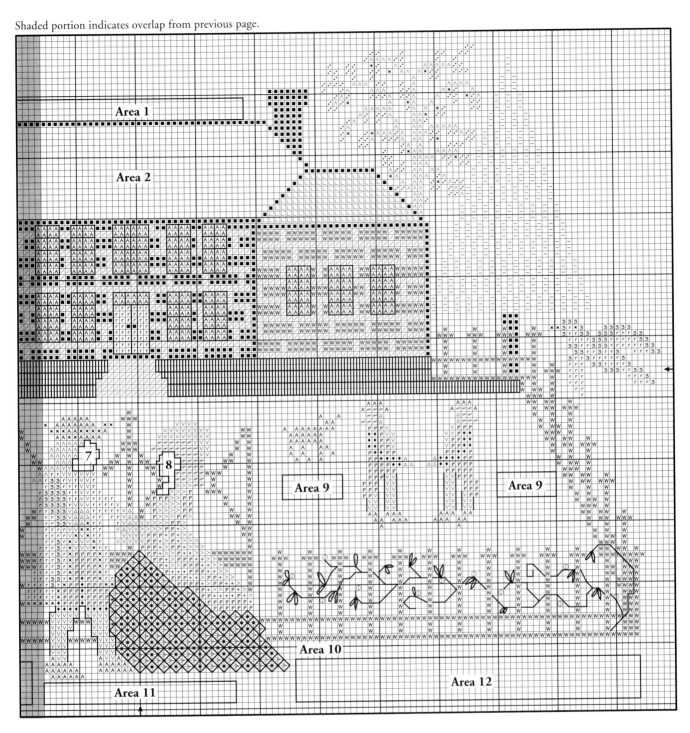

Area 1

Area 2

Area 9

Area 9

Area 7

Area 8

7

8

Area 10

Area 11

Area 12

Instructions: Cross stitch over two threads, using one strand of silk. Backstitch using one strand of silk. Make specialty stitches using one strand of silk.

Backstitch instructions:

Top panel

3831	3033	2613	windowpanes, man's socks
2126	935	—	vines
3344	3790	2609	door
4113	422	2673	boys' legs

Front panel

#5 Japan Gold   gate, embroidery hoops

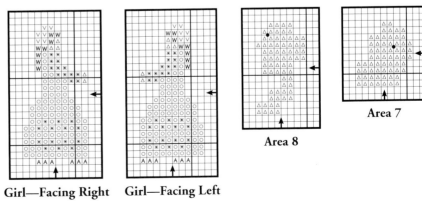

Girl—Facing Right   **Girl—Facing Left**

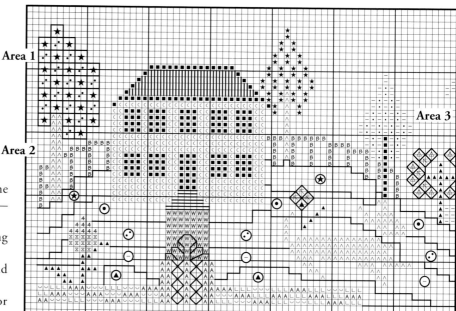

Area 1

Area 2

Area 3

FRONT PANEL

Special instructions:

Top panel

Area 1: Cross stitch surname over one thread, using one strand 2126/935/— and alphabet provided.

Area 2: Work herringbone stitch using one strand 3416/—/—.

Area 3: Work satin stitch using one strand 1835/3363/2469.

Areas 4 & 10: Work queen stitch for woman's dress and plants in garden.

Area 5: Work lazy-daisy stitch using one strand 2126/935/—.

Area 6: Work bullion knots where symbol ⊕ appears in vine, using one strand 3335/208/2532.

Areas 7 & 8: Cross stitch over one thread, using one strand of silk. Make French knot for eye where • appears at intersecting grid lines, using one strand 3842/415/2415 and wrapping silk around needle twice.

Area 9: Cross stitch children's initials over one thread, using one strand 1835/3363/2469 and alphabet provided.

Area 11: Cross stitch couple's initials over one thread, using one strand 4233/437/2738 and alphabet provided.

Area 12: Cross stitch ancestor's initials over two threads, alternating between colors 1715/930/2930 and 934/350/2350.

Grape panel

Area 1: Work satin stitch using one strand 4232/543/2948, stitching in direction indicated by lines on chart.

Area 2: Work queen stitch for flowers.

Area 3: Work satin stitch using one strand 3335/208/2532 for grape centers, stitching in direction indicated by lines on chart.

Area 4: Work satin stitch using one strand 3024/3350/2327 for grape centers, stitching in direction indicated by lines on chart.

Area 5: Work satin stitch using one strand 3323/3042/— for grape centers, stitching in direction indicated by lines on chart.

Area 6: Work queen stitch for basket.

Strawberry panel

Area 1: Work Florentine stitch over four threads, referring to chart on page 60 for color placement.

Area 2: Work queen stitch for strawberries.

Area 3: Work eyelet stitch for design in basket.

Front panel

Area 1: Work rice stitch for tree.

Area 2: Work satin stitch using one strand 3344/3790/2609 for roof of house and one strand 2231/3046/2673 for steps of

house, stitching in direction indicated by lines on chart. Work satin stitch for grass according to color-code symbols, stitching vertically.

Area 3: Work queen stitch for flowers.

Area 4: Work bullion knots where symbol ⊙ appears using one strand 931/352/2352 and where symbol ⊗ appears using one strand 2231/3046/2673.

Back panel

Area 1: Work satin stitch using one strand 1835/3363/2469 for base of roses, stitching in direction indicated by lines on chart.

Area 2: Work four-sided stitch using one strand 1714/931/2931.

Shaded portion indicates overlap from previous page.

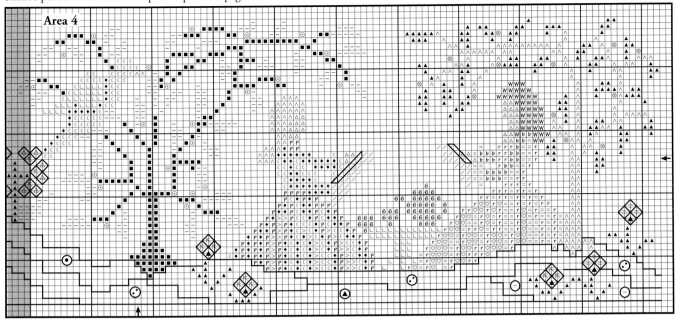

Area 4

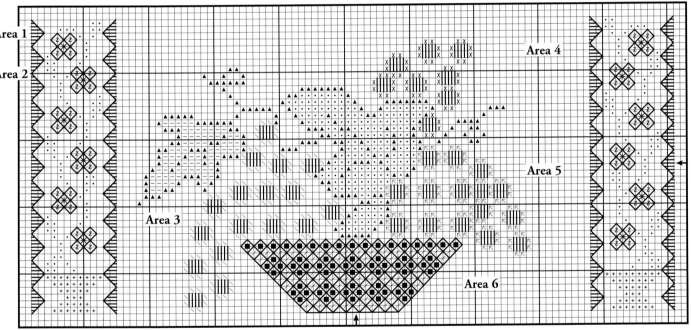

Area 1

Area 2

Area 4

Area 3

Area 5

Area 6

GRAPE PANEL

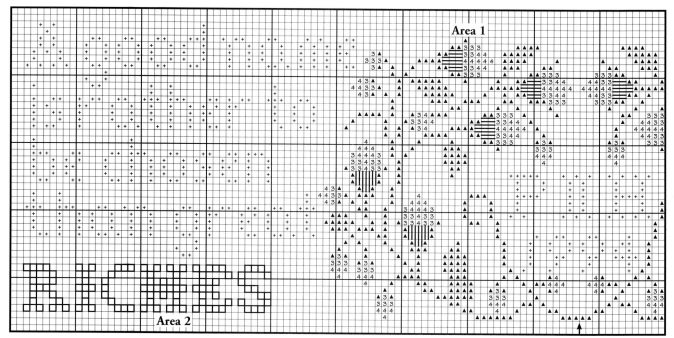

Area 1

Area 2

BACK PANEL

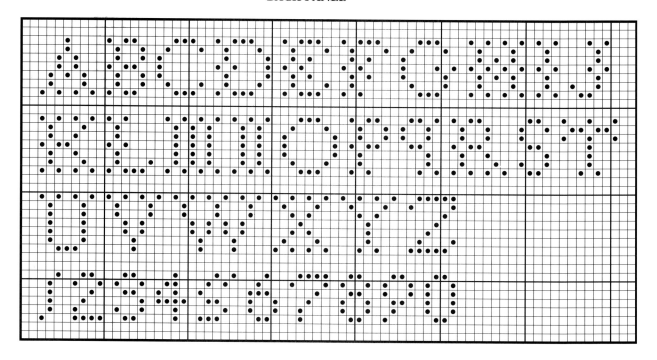

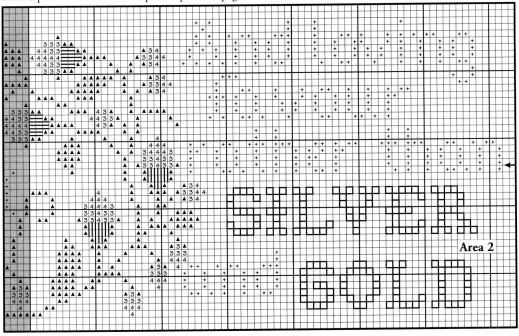

Area 2

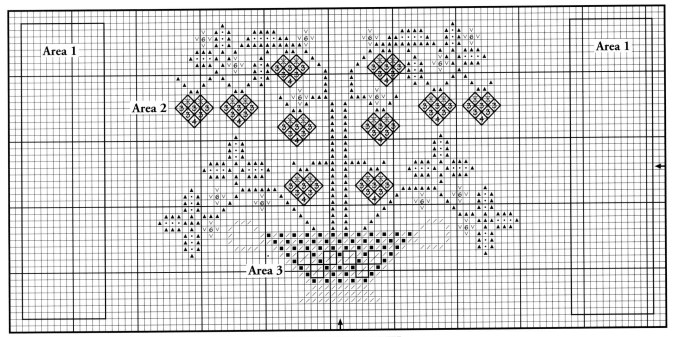

Area 1

Area 1

Area 2

Area 3

STRAWBERRY PANEL

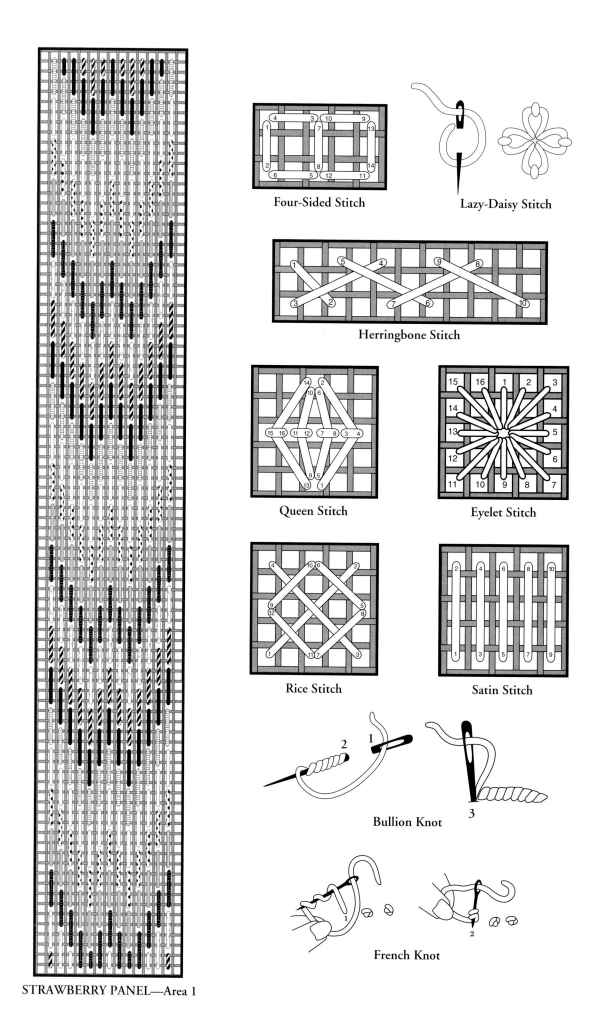

STRAWBERRY PANEL—Area 1

Four-Sided Stitch

Lazy-Daisy Stitch

Herringbone Stitch

Queen Stitch

Eyelet Stitch

Rice Stitch

Satin Stitch

Bullion Knot

French Knot

and thos that shall inquir. . . .

An Historical Survey of Seventeenth-Century Needlework Cabinets

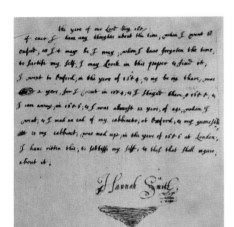

*T*he *yere of our Lord bᵉing 1657:
if ever I have any thoughts about the
time; when I went to Oxford; as It may
be I may; when I have forgotten the time;
to sartifi my self; I may Loock in this
paper & find it; I went to Oxford; in the
yere of 1654; & my be ing there; near
. . . 2 yers; for I went in 1654; & I
stayed there; 1655; & I cam away; in
1656; & I was allmost 12 yers; of age;
when I went; & I mad an end of my
cabbinete; at Oxford; & my quenesᵗh;
. . . & my cabbinet; was mad up; in the
yere of 1656 at London; I have ritten
this; to sartisfi my self; & thos that
shall inquir; about it;*

                                    Hannah Smith

A written legacy from the hand of a young, seventeenth-century embroideress was placed in her completed needlework cabinet for "thos that shall inquir; about it." It would appear as though she foresaw a time when she would wish to recall her own experiences and bequeathed a narrative for those yet to come. Through this unusually conscientious forethought, needlework historians have been given a valuable glimpse into the life of this young girl. Because of this rare and reflective documentation, we can also gain insight into the importance placed upon the needle arts as they applied to the educational development of young ladies.

Students of historical embroidery realize that the artifacts we so cherish today are much more than mere combinations of the materials and stitching techniques that comprise each work. They often offer a splendid perspective of the economic, religious, political, and socialization processes that were implemented through the educational practices of their time. If we can find and understand these interconnecting relationships, those embroideries given to our care can be better appreciated.

The Stuart Era in England lasted a little over one hundred years, from 1603 until 1714. It was during this time that Britain experienced prodigious and far-reaching changes in both its social and its political structures. The reign of Charles I and Queen Henrietta, the Puritan Commonwealth under Cromwell, and finally the Restoration of Charles II and Queen Catherine of Braganza all played a vital role in that evolutionary development. It was during this period of change that England became a major world power, engaged in the beginnings of a parliamentary form of government, and set into motion revolutions in science, religion, and philosophy. With these rapid changes and upheavals taking place, one might think the simple amusement of needle and thread might suffer. On the contrary, professional and domestic embroidery evolved and flourished during this time. One major contributing factor was the rise of the merchant and upper-middle classes, some of whom eventually developed into the status of landed gentry. By combining the desire to exhibit this newfound prosperity within their domestic surroundings and the socialization process of educating their young daughters in the prescribed accomplishments, a wealth of polychrome samplers, needlelace samplers, tent-work pictures, book bindings, beaded baskets, raised-work pictures, silk-work pictures, mirror frames, pincushions, and cabinets of needlework were created. These embroideries were worked by young girls who came from many diverse backgrounds. They were the daughters of the landed gentry, upper-middle-class merchants, ministers, and skilled craftsmen.

During this time, the academic education of a girl's development was not emphasized to any great degree as it was for the male population. Whether a young lady was tutored at home or within a school setting, her training was generally limited to religious instruction, social skills, and domestic accomplishments of which the needle played a paramount role. A girl could be taught needlework skills in a structured home setting, attend an established school, or be guided by the hands of a skilled needlewoman. A passage in the diary (1644–1657) of Ralph Josselin, Vicar of Earl Colne, Essex, states, "Both these

*E*mbroidered cabinet (1650–1660). *Allegorical group representing the five senses. Accented with floral and animal forms. Laid and couched silk embroidered upon a fine, linen ground, highlighted with seed pearls and trimmed in silver braid. 12" high x 10" wide x 7½" deep. The Examplarery collection.*

Figure 1

Figure 2

Figure 3

Figure 5

Figure 4

Figure 8

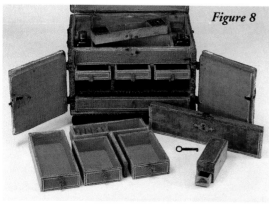

Figure 6

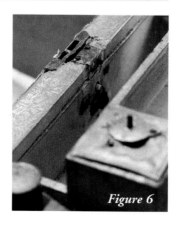

Figure 7

weeks God was good to me and mine in our health. . . . Mary was out at Mrs. Elliston's, where she learned to sew; [sic]"

"A Cabinett is such as Ladys keep their rings, necklaces, Braceletts and jewells in. It stands on the table (called a dressing table) in their bed chamber," so described Randall Holme in *The Academy of Armory* in 1688.

These embroidered boxes and cabinets span the entire seventeenth century, taking various styles and forms and employing many different needlework techniques. Generally most of those that have survived date from the 1640s until the end of the century. While styles overlapped during this period, the earliest examples at the beginning of the century appear to have been oblong, with either a flat or a padded top. These boxes were sometimes constructed with a set of compartments and drawers. Toward the middle of this period, an elegant top with canted sides, hinged to a rectangular, lower base containing many small drawers came into vogue and appeared mostly during a period spanning twenty years and lasting from the 1650s to the early 1670s (Figure 1). These were the most visually pleasing and intricately constructed of the cabinets. In such elaborate receptacles could be placed feminine toiletries, writing implements, letters, personal valuables, cherished trinkets, and perhaps the instruments and materials for performing needlework activities. The uppermost lid opened to reveal a silk-lined, rectangular chamber that, when lifted out, might reveal a paneled compartment lined with a quicksilver looking glass (Figure 2). This form of mirrored glass was quite new to the manufacturing industry in Britain during the seventeenth century and was very highly valued. Often in this compartment, a grouping of figures and miniature trees was placed, forming a tiny garden or a pastoral scene. From this top, the canted sides were paneled down to the lower base and carried a variety of embroidered pictorial, geometric, and floral bands. When the hinged, upper portion was unlocked, it revealed the lower base, which contained a deep, inner compartment or well (Figure 3). The lid of this hinged section often

carried a looking glass that was fastened down with metal claws. This deep area was sectioned off with space to hold writing implements and with slots for paper. There were also divisions that had padded cushions and areas that had sliding panels that concealed small, shallow areas (Figure 4). The sunken, front tray was fitted with furnishings of two glass scent bottles, an inkwell, a pounce box, and/or sand caster. In front of this large, welled area was an arrangement of drawers: a wide panel containing the lock above a series of three small drawers, ending with a lower drawer across the bottom (Figure 5). This locked panel could be slid up and out by removing the sunken tray and pressing the back of a locking mechanism (Figure 6). Revealed, then, were three small drawers. Upon removal and comparison of these three drawers, it was usually found that two of the drawers were of a different length than the remaining section. The shorter one of the three provided an area behind for yet another drawer to rest. This fourth drawer had been crafted with a divider that ran between the other three sections (Figure 7). After being carefully removed, the divider revealed a horizontal compartment that was lined in velvet and slotted for placing rings (Figure 8). The inside of the cabinet was then protected by another hinged door, which dropped open from the top, or by two doors that opened to the right and left. Other examples exist that were constructed with a solid front

that did not open. An interesting point is that in a comparison of the interiors, this particular style of cabinet tended to use the same concealed or "secret" compartments in a similar manner from one box to the next. By the third quarter of the century, the stepped style was no longer the prevailing fashion and the cabinets once again reverted to the simple, oblong form (Figure 9).

Subject matter and stitching techniques used on these boxes generally tended to reflect the fashion practiced on other forms of contemporary embroidery. Needlework historians recognize that since many of these patterns and motifs were repeated on cabinets, tent-stitch pictures, and mirrored frames, the design elements would have been procured—pre-drawn on fine linen or thick, white satin—from, perhaps, a printseller or professional pattern drawers.

The printseller sold sheets of engravings in a variety of styles and themes and was a very important part of the economy in the arena of decorative arts. These engravers and printsellers also provided designs for others working in a wide variety of fields. Woodworkers, silversmiths, stone-carvers, and painters all sought the services of the printseller.

Flat-topped cabinet (second quarter of the seventeenth century). Silk and metal threads upon a satin ground, accented with spangles (oes). Photograph courtesy of Stephen & Carol Huber.

Figure 9

Figure 10

Side-panel detail from a cabinet, depicting the hanging of Haman, worked in laid and couched silk threads upon a silk ground. Entire piece edged with metal braid. Figure measures 3½" high x 1½" wide. Panel measures 4½" high x 14" wide. The Examplarery collection.

The acquisition of pre-drawn designs would also explain why there tended to be some regularity in the scale of the various scenes and motifs over a wide range of embroideries. Whereas, if the needleworker or other draftsman transferred directly from a variety of different sources, using a pouncing transfer technique, there would be a noticeable size variance to the composition. This method of direct transfer would have been more successfully used to create canvas-work pictures and cushions rather than for cabinets. Uncut, pre-drawn panels in various stages of needlework completion for cabinets and mirror frames can still be found today. The design elements upon these pieces were placed very close together. Once completed, they were cut apart and applied to the desired form and the edges were covered with silver gimp.

Designs for cabinets could have been obtained from noted London engravers and printsellers such as Peter Stent, John Overton, Robert Walton, and others. Peter Stent made note of more than five hundred titles in his 1662 trade list. He published from the year 1643 to 1667 at the Sign of the White Horse on Giltspur Street. John Overton distributed his wares at the White Horse Inn in Little Britain next door to Little Saint Bartholomew's Gate and also at the White Horse without New Gate at the corner of the Little Old

Bailey from 1667 to 1707. Titles such as *A Book of Flowers, Fruits, Beasts, Birds and Flies . . .* and *The second booke of Flowers . . . exactly drawne, newly printed with additions by John Dunstal, 1661* were but two of the more popular publications of the time that depicted objects that could easily be adapted to embroidery. Other prominent titles drawn upon for their illustrations were also available as *The Five Senses; Marmion Inventer; The Four Elements, Fire, Air, Earth and Water; Pictures lately printed in sheet;* and *King Charles the First,* to name but a few. Many of the designs found in these books were borrowed from even earlier works, such as Edward Topsell's *Historie of Four-Footed Beasts,* published in 1607. Small motifs used on the narrower panels of the cabinets could very well have been copied directly from this publication. The larger design elements were drawn from other engraved sources. According to J. L. Nevinson in his article *Peter Stent and John Overton, Publishers of Embroidery designs . . . Apollo, 1936,* "Where each plate bears the printer's and publisher's imprint one is justified in concluding that the sheets could be sold separately or at any rate were not expected to stay together."

In 1671, Overton offered, "Four hundred new sorts of Birds, Beasts, Flowers, Fruits, Fish, Flyes, Worms, Landskips, Ovals and Histories, etc. Lively

coloured for all sorts of Gentlewomen and School-Mistresses Work."

It is also noted by Margaret Swain in *Embroidered Stuart Pictures* that one designer and supplier of pre-drawn designs was John Nelham, a member of the Broderers' Company of London. He supplied illustrations and signed both his name and place of business on some of his works, thusly: *JNO NELHAM, SUGAR LOFE, GRETFRIARS, NEWGATE MARKET.* John Nelham and his father, Roger Nelham, each left a collection of "prints" when they died. According to his will, dated 1653, Roger left to his son John: "the halfe of my books and prints and patterns which I do use for the drawing of workes . . . All my beams and lathes and working instruments which do appertain and belong to my worke house."

Designs used on cabinets were generally comprised of themes of an historical, social, religious, or mythological nature. Illustrations depicting political events were often not very popular embroidery themes prior to the seventeenth century. However, the period of violence surrounding the brief reign of Charles I influenced both style and subject during this time. Portraits of Stuart kings and queens dressed in contemporary garments tended to replace mythological rulers and heroes of antiquity (Figure 10). Religious controversy increased the desire for biblical themes, replacing old mythological tales considered to be lacking in moral value. Biblical figures were placed on a background with rolling hills, windmills, houses, and formal gardens situated among both rare and domestic animals. Such compositions "reveal Stuart society's ability to combine divided worlds, passing freely from the timeless sphere of biblical history to contemporary life," states Yvonne Hackenbroch in *English and other Needlework Tapestries and Textiles In the Untermyer Collection.*

"These stories will be seen mostly to portray such feminine themes as maternity and fertility; less predictable perhaps is the representation by Seventeenth Century English gentlewomen of violence, retribution and female supremacy," states Mary Gostelow in *Art of Embroidery.*

Many of the religious designs were taken from the engraved plates found in

Thesacarum Historiarum Veteris Testamenti of Gerard de Jode, a volume of Bible illustrations published in Antwerp in 1589. Old Testament themes such as Rebekah, Solomon and the Queen of Sheba, Esther and King Ahazuerus, and Susannah and the Elders were all quite popular. The lid panel of Hannah Smith's cabinet shows *"Joseph raised from the pit and sold by his brothers to the Midianite merchants"* taken from an engraving of de Jode.

Due to the contributions of such esteemed needlework historians as Margaret Swain, Santina Levey, J. L. Nevinson, Nancy Cabot, and Xanthe Brooke, many old assumptions concerning various aspects of seventeenth-century needlework have been changed. Thus, research "has dispelled the myth that the domestic needlewoman created her own designs by copying the flowers, birds and other creatures of her own garden. By the middle of the Seventeenth Century she was well provided for by the large number of engravings available for the sale in printseller's and booksellers' shop." So states Dr. Jennifer Harris, curator of textiles at the Whitworth Art Gallery, Manchester, England, in an article that appeared in the July 1988 issue of *The Antique Collector,* a British magazine.

At various periods during the seventeenth century, the cabinets tended to have been completed in three popular needlework techniques of flat stitch (laid or couched), canvas work (tent stitch), and raised work (stumpwork). A. F. Kendrick, in *English Needlework,* relates that "stumpwork cabinets go back as far as the reign of Charles I. Dated examples of raised work and flat stitching run concurrently through the Seventeenth Century."

A variety of stitching techniques and materials enhanced these three major categories for the exteriors of these cabinets. Incorporated within the work can be found queen stitch, encroaching gobelin stitch, long and short stitches, French knots, padded-lace stitches, split and stem stitches, detached buttonhole stitch, flossed paper (gum work), applied canvas motifs (slips), cut silk pile, and couched and laid work. The materials with which such techniques were executed range from varieties of silks,

spangles (oes, known as sequins during modern times), seed pearls, metal purl, mica, gold thread, glass beads, looped metal thread, chenille, and silver braid.

The materials for a wide variety of needlework activities could have been obtained at a central location in London. Established in 1566 in Cornhill on Threadneedle Street was a commercial hub known as the Royal Exchange. A variety of business activities and commodities could be obtained from merchants and tradesmen. Surrounding a central courtyard, the building housed milliners, booksellers, goldsmiths, and apothecaries. According to social historian Kathleen Epstein, textile materials and related services were available at the Royal Exchange, as supported by primary source references in the literature of the day.

The interiors of the cabinets tended to be finished quite simply, in velvet, or with geometric patterns worked over vellum strips, using long stitches. For such an example of this geometric treatment, see the embroidered cabinet, New England or England, 1657–1685, in *Girlhood Embroidery: American Samplers & Pictorial Needlework 1650–1850* by Betty Ring. Although found on the exterior panels, these geometrically worked long stitches were generally reserved for the interiors, where less wear or friction would occur. It has been suggested that

such strips could have been obtained at the place where the cabinet was completed, rather than being worked by the embroideress. Few examples had the interiors elaborately and painstakingly embroidered.

". . . and my quenest᷎h; . . . & my cabinet; was mad up; in the yere of 1656 at London; . . ." So wrote Hannah Smith. This written documentation tends to support the fact that when the panels were completed, the work was returned to a professional for finishing. To date, we do not have enough primary source materials that would positively identify exactly where, or to whom, the panels might have been returned. One possible source for finishing could have been that of John Overton. Printed on the base of a tray in a flat-topped box can be found: *SOLD BY JOHN OVERTON AT THE SIGN OF THE WHITE HORSE INN.* We can only speculate as to whether or not the completed embroidered panels

Embroidered cabinet by Hannah Smith (1654–1656). Worked on a canvas and satin ground using laid, raised, and canvas stitches in silk, metal threads, seed pearls, and spangles (oes). 12" high x 10" wide x 7" deep. Whitworth Art Gallery, University of Manchester.

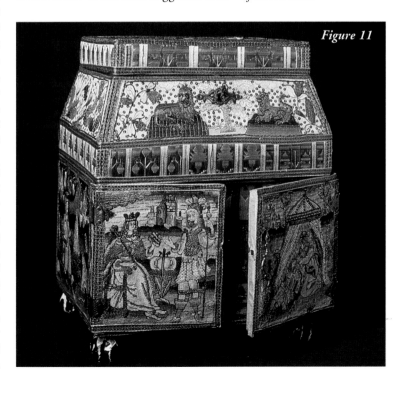

Figure 11

were returned to the establishment where the pre-drawn pattern was acquired. Perhaps from this point, the work was then subcontracted to a cabinetmaker or to an upholsterer.

To complete the box, the panels were affixed to the wooden cabinet form and edged with metal thread (gimp). The interior was often lined with red, blue, or salmon pink silk and occasionally with green or yellow silk. The exposed wooden edges were covered with embossed paper. It was then fitted with accoutrements of glass scent bottles, a sand dredger, and a pounce box. Silver-plated or metal

Embroidered cabinet of Martha Edlin. Initialed ME 1671. Worked upon satin and canvas ground in laid, raised, and canvas stitches, using silk and metal threads. Accented with seed pearls and edged with silver braid. 9½" high x 11¾" wide x 10" deep. By courtesy of the Trustees of the Victoria & Albert Museum.

handles and escutcheons were then added. Cabinets toward the later part of the century had panels formed in tortoiseshell, which coincided with the framing methods found on embroidered mirror frames. The entire cabinet rested upon four ball feet made from a variety of materials, such as wood or silver. Surviving examples show that there was normally an accompanying wooden or leather box in which to carry the cabinet.

The needle arts were held in very high esteem as an important element of a young lady's educational training. During the seventeenth century, it was not frowned upon as an idle occupation. Rozsika Parker in *The Subversive Stitch* relates, "It has been stated that little girls were instructed to be little women and embroidery was a constant in their lives that linked childhood to womanhood. It taught obedience and patience over technically complex and demanding patterns."

Although professional examples of embroideries were executed in the various categories discussed so far, there

have been left to us the documented works of two young girls, Hannah Smith and Martha Edlin.

Hannah Smith's cabinet (1654–1656) is in the form of a stepped top with sloping, canted sides. At approximately twelve years of age, she embellished her richly embroidered piece in a variety of different techniques, employing canvas work, flat silk, and raised work (Figure 11). The front door panels are worked in tent and queen stitches on a canvas ground. On the left door panel, we find Deborah and Barak and on the right door panel, we find Jael and Siser scenes adapted from the Old Testament. The side panels are embroidered using laid satin stitch as well as long and short stitches in scenes representative of summer and winter. The lid panel portrays, *"Joseph raised from the pit and sold by his brothers to the Midianite merchants."* The figure of Joseph is embroidered in raised work. On the front, canted panels we find representations of a lion and leopard that are also worked in this raised technique. The back of the cabinet is stitched with geometric laid-silk work. The entire piece is executed in silk, metal threads, seed pearls, and spangles.

Perhaps the most crowning element to this piece is the documentation of Hannah's work through her written legacy. For needlework historians, this note is more than just a recording of dates, places, and accomplishments; it also provides evidence that this child had been taught to write. The ability to write was not a universal skill acquired by the majority of women at that time. Epstein states that more than ninety percent of seventeenth-century English women could not write or sign their names. It was believed that the ability to read the Bible was crucial for one's salvation; and therefore, the mastery of these skills was very important to a young girl's education. The skill necessary to translate thoughts and experiences to paper, however, was more closely linked to occupational needs and, therefore, was considered more important for the male population.

Another documented group left to us contains the works of Martha Edlin. Her completed pieces were executed between the ages of eight and thirteen

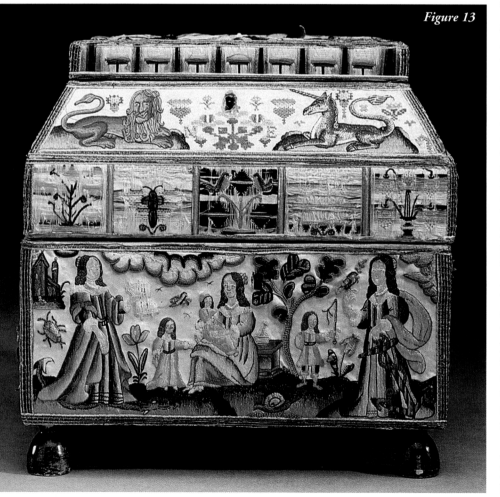

Figure 13

(1668–1673). According to family letters, Martha was born in 1660. The cabinet and its contents were passed down through the female line of the family and were then acquired by the Victoria & Albert Museum in 1990. Because the various pieces of embroidery contained within her cabinet were initialed and dated, one can see the progression of needlework skills that were nurtured within this child (Figure 12).

It would appear that the chronology of this body of work demonstrates the fact that embroidered cabinets were the ultimate culmination of a young lady's needlework training. We have also been given this wonderful progression of designs from which we can better judge the length of time it commanded to complete a particular element. For example, at the age of eight, Martha executed a polychrome silk sampler in an elaborate and banded series of patterns. It was signed and dated in 1668. Her whitework sampler was worked on a linen that had a very deep yellow hue and contained four intricate bands of white thread embroidery and three bands of complex, openwork lace patterns. It was dated one year later in 1669.

Her exquisite cabinet was accomplished within a two-year period and was initialed and dated 1671 (Figure 13). The panels of white satin were worked in flat and raised work, using silk, chenille, coiled wire, and metal threads, and were accented with seed pearls. The lid panel represents music in the form of a seated figure with a lute, worked in tent stitch with detached needlepoint lace. The four corners contain representations of the four elements: earth, air, fire, and water. On the angled sides, animal designs are worked in the form of a lion, a unicorn, a camel, a leopard, an elephant, a stag, a hound, and a rabbit. The figures are separated by stylized sprays of flowers. The lower portion of the cabinet shows a representation of the Seven Virtues. On the front panel appear Faith, Hope, and Charity. Justice, Temperance, Fortitude, and Prudence appear on the two side panels. The back was worked in tent stitch in the form of a hunting scene. The inside of the box was fitted with a looking glass and a scent bottle and was lined with salmon pink silk.

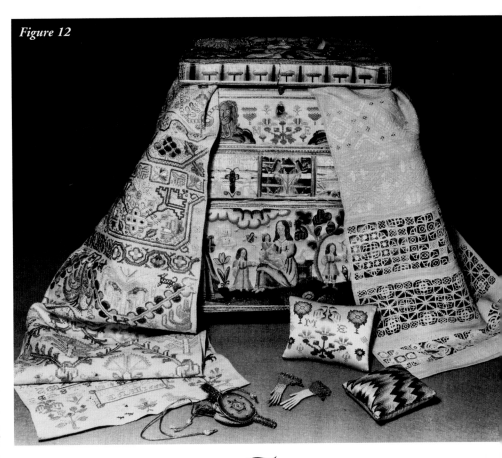

Figure 12

Contained in the cabinet were many small articles such as pincushions, a needlecase, a scent bellow, a miniature pair of gloves, and a group of silver miniatures in the forms of a candlestick, a chocolate pot, a teapot, a salver, a snuffer, a covered cooking pan, and a saucepan, all marked *ME*. In a special, concealed area of the cabinet were found two lockets: one with a portrait of King Charles II and the other with a representation of Cupid. Also found was an initialed bodkin, a tiny seal, and a small box containing a set of spoons, forks, and triangular saltcellars. To complete her accomplishments, a beaded jewel case was worked on a satin ground with silk, using tent stitch, couched work, and queen stitch, with a central, encircled medallion with a ribbon-like, raised, and looped border. It was worked in 1673. The work of Martha Edlin was described at length in a wonderful article by Leigh Ashton, which was published in *Connoisseur,* July 1928.

In this survey of embroidered cabinets, we found that many outside factors influenced the designs of seventeenth-century needlework. Economic, religious, and political forces were rapidly

The cabinet and embroidered contents (1668–1671) completed by Martha Edlin. Cabinet, whitework sampler, polychrome sampler, pincushions, scent bellow, and miniature gloves. By courtesy of the Trustees of the Victoria & Albert Museum.

evolving during this time. Due to these fluctuating forces, the fabric of the Stuart era was in constant change. The needle arts intertwined and mirrored the various forces at work that were so rapidly transforming society. The elegant cabinets we have surveyed should, therefore, be looked upon as more than just pleasant diversions. We should savor the qualities of these charming specimens, keeping in mind that each was the culmination of a young lady's training. They are examples from which we can derive pleasure in their visual beauty, from which we can be entertained by their sometimes whimsical portrayal of classical themes, and from which we can marvel at the tenacity and fortitude displayed through the work of these very accomplished young ladies.

Marriage Sampler

Simple elegance best describes this eye-catching sampler. Fashioned using many of the elements that are common to samplers of the past, this stitchery will be cherished by its owner, both for its beauty and for the message it conveys. A meandering border encloses the central design, which includes a popular verse from First Corinthians. Floral wreaths encircle the names of the bride and groom, and space has been included for marking the date of their marriage. The colors used can be adapted to complement the room in which the completed sampler will be displayed, making this timeless design a decorative treasure to the couple for whom it is stitched.

Area 1

Area 3

Area 2

Area 4

Area 3

Area 5

Area 6

Area 7

Marriage Sampler

▲ 500 2500 1845 blue green, vy. dk.

Fabric: 32-count light mocha Belfast linen from Zweigart®
Stitch count: 217H x 217W
Design size:

18-count	12" x 12"
28-count	15½" x 15½"
32-count	13½" x 13½"
36-count	12" x 12"

Instructions: Cross stitch over two threads, using two strands of floss. Backstitch year using one strand 930/2930/1715.

Special instructions:
Area 1: Work four-sided stitch for top and sides of inner border, using one strand 930/2930/1715.

Area 2: Cross stitch over one thread, using one strand of floss.

Areas 3 & 4: Cross stitch names over one thread, using one strand of floss and alphabet provided.

Area 5: Cross stitch date over one thread, using one strand of floss.

Area 6: Work queen stitch using one strand of floss.

Area 7: Work satin stitch for bottom of inner border, using two strands 822/2644/3811.

	DMC	Kreinik	
	DMC	FT	Soie d'Alger	
⌐	822	2644	3811	beige-gray, lt.
∟	224	2223	4621	pink, lt.
‖	224	2223	4621	pink, lt.
○	223	2222	4622	pink, med.
M	3721	2221	4623	pink, dk.
L	676	2673	2243	old gold, lt.
△	729	2783	2242	old gold, med.
■	680	2782	2235	old gold, dk.
••	3753	2933	1712	antique blue, ul. vy. lt.
✘	932	2932	1713	antique blue, lt.
•	930	2930	1715	antique blue, dk.
ℓ	320	2320	1833	pistachio, med.
ϗ	367	2320	1834	pistachio, dk.

Shaded portion indicates overlap from previous page and page 71.

Area 4

Area 5

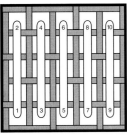

Satin Stitch

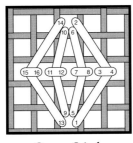

Queen Stitch

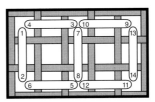

Four-Sided Stitch

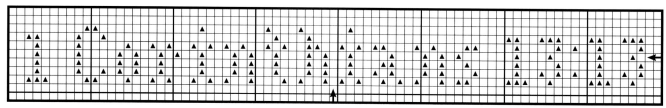

Area 2

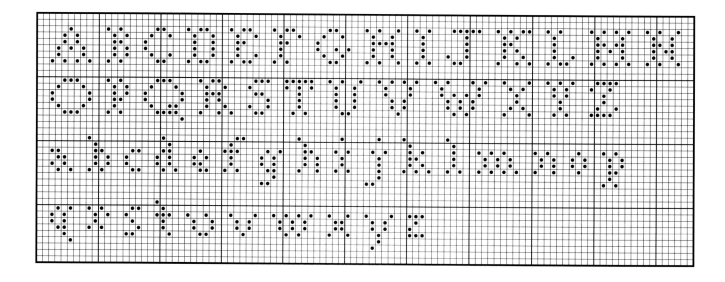

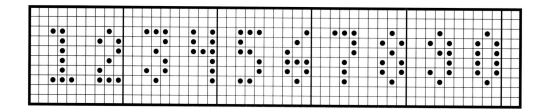

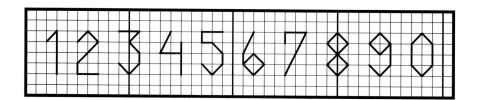

Greek-Key Sampler

This appealing design presents a variety of popular sampler motifs from needlework of the past, in a delightful and charming design that will be a pleasure to stitch. Within the border is a variety of stitches worked to form this attractive design. A single alphabet and a trio of crowns are encompassed by a Greek-key pattern at the top of the sampler while below is included a lovely, floral dividing band that takes its inspiration from the winding floral bands of the nineteenth century and earlier. Colorful queen stitches form another band, and the remainder of the piece is completed with a block of bargello, or Florentine stitch, acorn motifs, a pair of stylized floral motifs, a band of numerals, and the designer's name and date. An alphabet and numerals chart is included for personalization.

This small, Greek-Key Sampler is a wonderfully colorful piece. Including modern-day versions of sampler motifs from the past, this design takes its roots from samplermaking history while leaving a legacy of modern-day needleart to historians of the future.

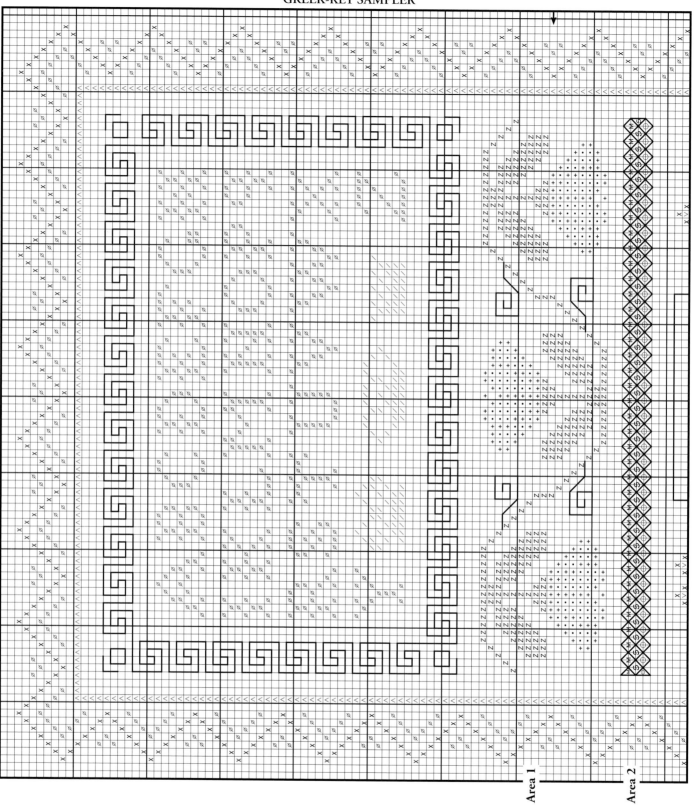

Area 1

Area 2

Shaded portion indicates overlap from previous page.

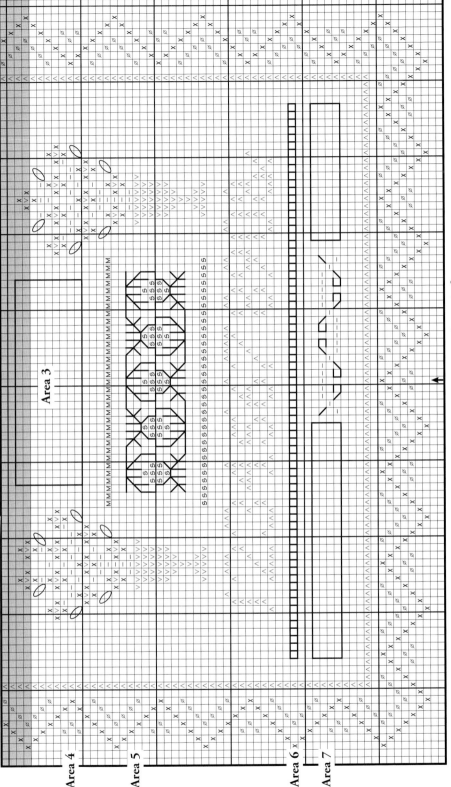

Greek-Key Sampler

	DMC	FT	Soie d'Alger	
○	221	2221	4624	pink, dk.
+	760	2760	2932	salmon
•	761	2761	2931	salmon, lt.
⌀	930	2930	1736	antique blue, dk.
∧	931	2931	1714	antique blue, med.
v	3045	2831	2242	yellow-beige, dk.
/	3046	2673	2243	yellow-beige, med.
Z	3363	2469	3723	pine green, med.
_	3364	2471	1831	pine green
S	3721	2221	4623	pink, dk.
M	3722	2221	4622	pink, med.
X	3750	2929	1716	antique blue, vy. dk.
▰▱	3721	2221	4623	pink, dk.
▱▱	3750	2929	1716	antique blue, vy. dk.
⬭	3045	2831	2242	yellow-beige, dk.
⬬	3363	2469	3723	pine green, med.
	3362	2937	3726	pine green, dk.

Fabric: 35-count antique white linen
Stitch count: 145H x 97W
Design size:

28-count	10⅜" x 7"
32-count	9" x 6"
35-count	8¼" x 5½"
40-count	7¼" x 4⅞"

Instructions: Cross stitch over two threads, using two strands of floss. Backstitch using one strand of floss.

Special instructions:

Inner Border: Work Bosnia stitch using two strands of floss.

Greek-Key Border: Work in backstitch or double running stitch, using one strand 221/2221/4624.

Area 1: Work double running stitch for tendrils, using one strand 3362/2937/3726.

Area 2: Work queen stitch using one strand of floss.

Area 3: Work bargello stitch using two strands of floss, referring to chart on page 78 for color placement.

Area 4: Work lazy-daisy stitch where symbol ⬭ appears, using two strands 3362/2937/3726.

Area 5: Work double running stitch for tendrils, using one strand 3721/2221/4623. Work Montenegrin stitch for band above acorn motif, using two strands of floss. Work long-armed cross stitch for band below acorn motif, using two strands of floss.

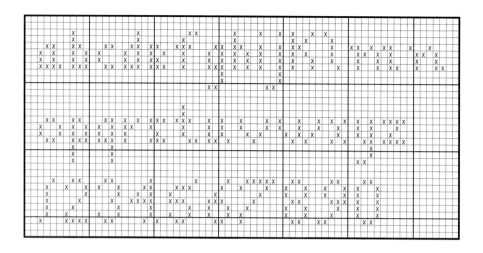

Area 6: Work four-sided stitch using one strand 221/2221/4624.

Area 7: Cross stitch name and date over one thread, using one strand 3750/2929/ 1716 and alphabet and numerals provided. Backstitch tendrils over one thread, using one strand 3363/2469/3723.

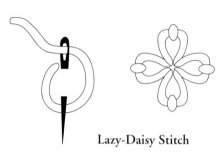

Lazy-Daisy Stitch

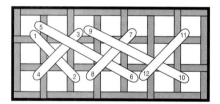

Long-Armed Cross Stitch

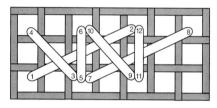

Montenegrin Stitch

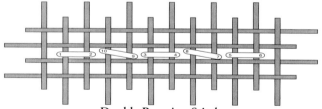

Double Running Stitch

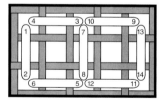

Four-Sided Stitch

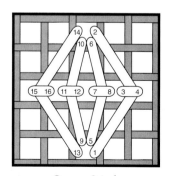

Queen Stitch

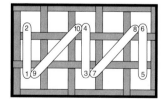

Bosnia Stitch

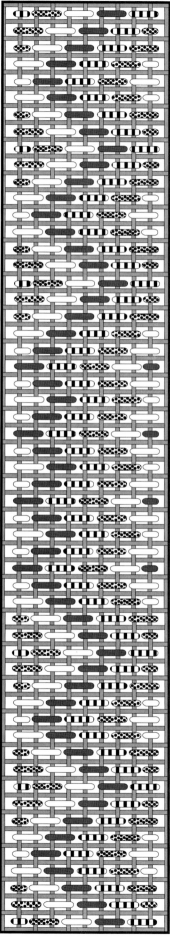

TOP

GREEK-KEY SAMPLER—Area 3

78

From the Heart Sampler

*T*he beauty of individuality will come shining through for each stitcher who works this engaging piece. Wrought using variegated, silk floss, the completed work will be different each time this design is stitched.

Muted floss colors and seed beads are artfully combined to create the magnificent *From the Heart Sampler*. A tribute to the art of the needle, this piece combines the artistry of samplers from the past with the distinct look achieved by using variegated floss. The color

of the floss is polychromatic, so the area within a skein that a stitcher chooses to begin working with will have a great effect on the finished appearance—no two needle artists will achieve exactly the same look on their completed work when using this fiber.

FROM THE HEART SAMPLER

Area 1

Area 2

Area 3

Area 4

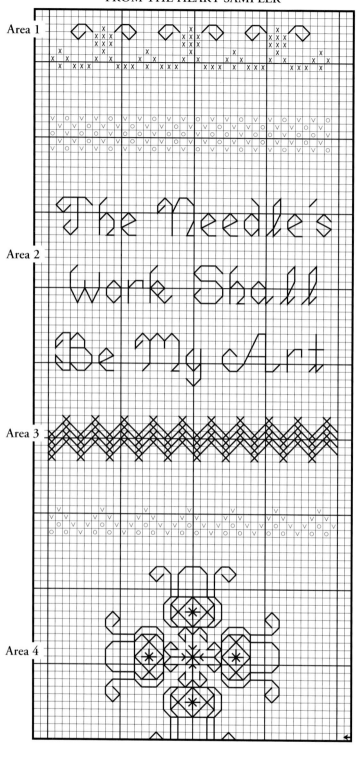

Shaded portion indicates overlap from chart at left.

Area 5

Area 6

Area 7

Area 8

Area 9

From the Heart Sampler

Caron
Waterlilies
X   Cafe Au Lait
v   Gobi Sand
S   Opal
     Navajo
     Cocoa

Mill Hill Seed Beads
O   161   Crystal

Fabric: 25-count cream Dublin linen from Zweigart®
Stitch count: 189H x 40W

Design size:

25-count	15⅛" x 3¼"
28-count	13½" x 2⅞"
32-count	11⅞" x 2½"
36-count	10½" x 2¼"

Instructions: Cross stitch over two threads, using two strands of silk. Backstitch using one strand of silk. Attach beads where symbol ○ appears, using one strand Opal and a half-cross stitch.

Special instructions:
Areas 1 & 9: Backstitch filigree using one strand Cafe Au Lait.
Areas 2 & 6: Backstitch verse using one strand Navajo.
Area 3: Work stacked herringbone stitch using two strands Opal for first row, two strands Gobi Sand for second row, two strands Cafe Au Lait for third row, and two strands Navajo for fourth row.
Area 4: Backstitch using one strand Cocoa.
Area 5: Work diamond eyelet stitch using two strands Opal. Work Algerian eye stitch using two strands Cafe Au Lait. Backstitch using one strand Cafe Au Lait.
Area 7: Backstitch filigree using one strand Cafe Au Lait. Work diamond eyelet stitch using two strands Gobi Sand.
Area 8: Backstitch using one strand Navajo. Personalize using alphabet and numerals provided.
NOTE: If your name is too long for the space provided, another line may be added before stitching final band of cross stitch.

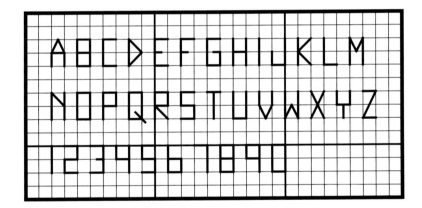

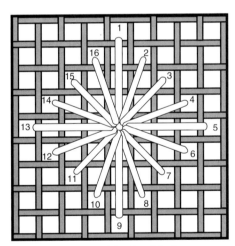

Diamond Eyelet Stitch

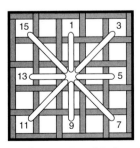

Algerian Eye Stitch

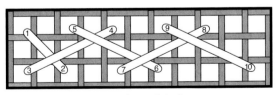

Herringbone Stitch

Harvest Sampler

The golden splendor of harvesttime comes to life in breathtaking stitchery in the extraordinary *Harvest Sampler*. A challenge to the enthusiastic needleworker, this incredible piece includes cross, back, Algerian eye, upright cross, diamond eyelet, Smyrna cross, plaited cross, straight and diagonal satin, herringbone, three-sided, barrier, long-armed cross, knitting, and lazy-daisy stitches. Completed using cotton embroidery floss, pearl cotton, and Marlitt fibers and accented with beads, this splendid design will grace the walls of any home in unforgettable style and will be a proud addition to the needleartist's collection of stitched masterpieces.

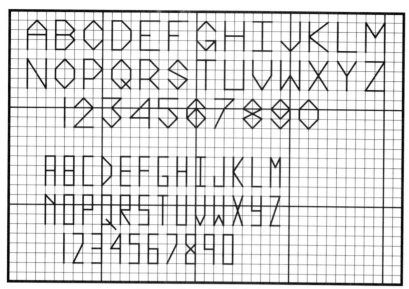

Harvest Sampler Alphabet

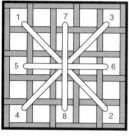

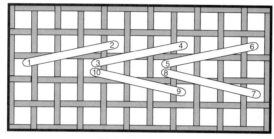

Smyrna Cross

Knitting Stitch

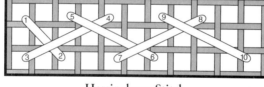

Herringbone Stitch

Lazy-Daisy Stitch

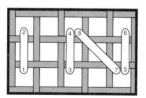
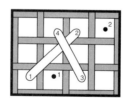

Barrier Stitch

Plaited Cross Stitch

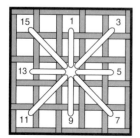

Algerian Eye Stitch

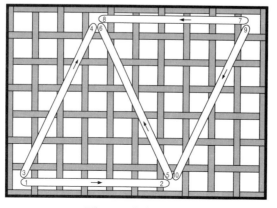

Three-Sided Stitch

Harvest Sampler

	DMC	Kreinik	
	DMC	FT	Soie d'Alger
••	ecru	ecru	F2	ecru
−	ecru	ecru	F2	ecru
	white	white	blanc	white
+	ecru	ecru	F2	ecru
	739	2738	4241	tan, ul. lt.
⌒	422	2673	3823	hazelnut, lt.
⊙	422	2673	3823	hazelnut, lt.
	3045	2831	3824	yellow-beige, dk.
ˌ	422	2673	3823	hazelnut, lt.
	739	2738	4241	tan, ul. lt.
Z	842	2842	3431	beige-brown, vy. lt.
✘	3032	2611	4534	mocha, med.
P	3041	—	4633	antique violet, med.
╱	372	2579	3833	mustard, lt.
	3013	2734	3721	khaki, lt.
└	371	2673	—	mustard
	3052	—	3714	green-gray, med.
ᗡ	370	2831	—	mustard, med.
	3363	2469	3723	pine green, med.
v	3042	—	4631	antique violet, lt.
	3041	—	4633	antique violet, med.
<	353	2352	921	peach flesh
	950	2950	2912	flesh, lt.
S	3773	2407	2913	flesh, med.
	3778	2356	2914	terra cotta, lt.
◖	3045	2831	3824	yellow-beige, dk.
	3782	2611	3831	mocha brown, lt.
X	3045	2831	3824	yellow-beige, dk.
bs	640	2640	3345	beige-gray, vy. dk.
bs	3740	—	4635	antique violet, dk.

DMC #12 Pearl Cotton (Coton Perlé)
ecru

Anchor® Marlitt
⊗   1037   old gold

Mill Hill Seed Beads
•   0557   Gold
¢   3005   Platinum Rose

Fabric: 28-count bone Brittney from Zweigart®
Stitch count: 193H x 144W
Design size:

25-count	15½" x 11½"
28-count	13¾" x 10¼"
32-count	12" x 9"
36-count	10¾" x 8"

Instructions: Cross stitch over two threads, using two strands of floss. Backstitch using one strand of floss unless otherwise indicated. When two colors are bracketed together, use one strand of each. When using Marlitt, use one strand.

Special instructions:

Outer border

1. Backstitch net pattern using Marlitt 1037.

2. Work diamond eyelet stitch using one strand each ecru/ecru/F2 and 739/2738/4241.

3. Work lazy-daisy clusters using one strand each 371/2673/— and 3052/—/3714 where symbol ◠ appears and one strand each 370/2831/— and 3363/2469/3723 where symbol ● appears.

4. Backstitch outside edge using one strand 640/2640/3345.

5. Attach gold Mill Hill seed beads where symbol ● appears, using one strand 422/2673/3823 and attaching after all other stitching has been completed.

NOTE: Blocks around small flowers are for placement purposes only and are not to be backstitched.

Serpentine rows

1. Backstitch serpentine motif using one strand each 422/2673/3823 and 3045/2831/3824 and then wrap using one strand Marlitt 1037.

2. Backstitch stems and make lazy-daisy leaves using one strand each 371/2673/— and 3052/—/3714.

3. Backstitch net pattern in medallions using one strand Marlitt 1037.

4. Work diamond eyelet stitch using one strand each ecru/ecru/F2 and 739/2738/4241.

5. Work Smyrna cross stitch near medallions, using one strand each ecru/ecru/F2 and 739/2738/4241 for center cross and one strand each 422/2673/3823 and 739/2738/4241 for remaining crosses.

NOTE: Blocks around small flowers are for placement purposes only and are not to be backstitched.

6. Above and below uppermost serpentine row, alternate Algerian eye stitches and anchored upright cross stitches using two strands 3045/2831/3824 for Algerian eye stitches and one strand each 422/2673/3823 and 739/2738/4241 for anchored upright cross stitches.

7. Above and below lowermost serpentine row, alternate Smyrna cross stitches and diamond eyelet stitches over four threads, using two strands 3045/2831/3824 for Smyrna crosses and one strand each 422/2673/3823 and 739/2738/4241 for diamond eyelets.

Wheat row

1. Straight stitch heads of wheat, using one strand each 422/2673/3823 and 3045/2831/3824.

2. Backstitch wheat stems, heads, and leaves using one strand 640/2640/3345.

3. Backstitch wheat fibers using one strand 3045/2831/3824.

Alphabet row

1. Backstitch where symbol ∨ appears, using one strand 3041/—/4633.

2. Backstitch where symbol P appears, using one strand 3740/—/4635.

3. Backstitch where symbol ⊙ appears, using one strand 640/2640/3345.

4. Backstitch the letter X using one strand 3740/—/4635.

Small-leaf row

1. Work diagonal satin stitch for thin lines, using one strand each 371/2673/— and 3052/—/3714.

2. Work diagonal satin stitch for thick lines, using one strand each 370/2831/— and 3363/2469/3723.

3. Backstitch stems using one strand 370/2831/—.

4. Attach Platinum Rose Mill Hill seed beads where symbol ¢ appears, using one strand 3773/2407/2913 and attaching after all other stitching has been completed.

Apple row

1. Backstitch leaves using one strand 370/2831/—.

2. Backstitch apples using one strand 640/2640/3345.

3. Backstitch stems using two strands 640/2640/3345.

Numeral row

Backstitch using one strand 3740/—/4635.

Date and initial blocks

1. Work plaited cross stitch in corners of both blocks, using one strand each 422/2673/3823 and 3045/2831/3824.

2. Work satin stitch using one strand each 422/2673/3823 and 739/2738/4241.

3. Backstitch initials and year using one strand each 371/2673/— and 3052/—/3714 and alphabet and numerals charts provided.

Row A: Work herringbone stitch using one strand ecru #12 Pearl Cotton.

Row B: Work three-sided stitch using one strand ecru #12 Pearl Cotton.

Row C: Work barrier stitch using one strand ecru #12 Pearl Cotton.

Row D: Work long-armed cross stitch using one strand pearl cotton.

Row E: Work horizontal knitting stitch using one strand pearl cotton.

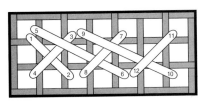

Long-Armed Cross Stitch

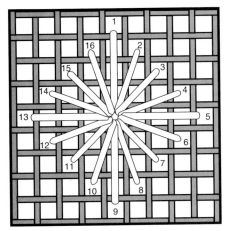

Diamond Eyelet Stitch

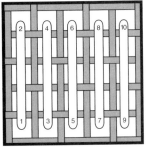

Satin Stitch—straight

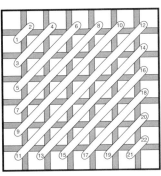

Satin Stitch—diagonal

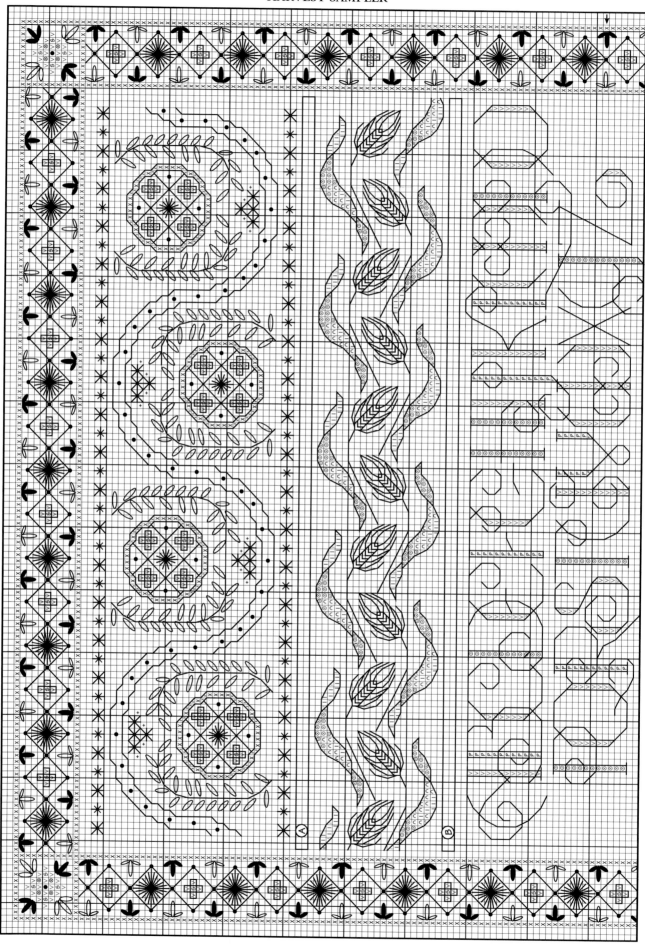

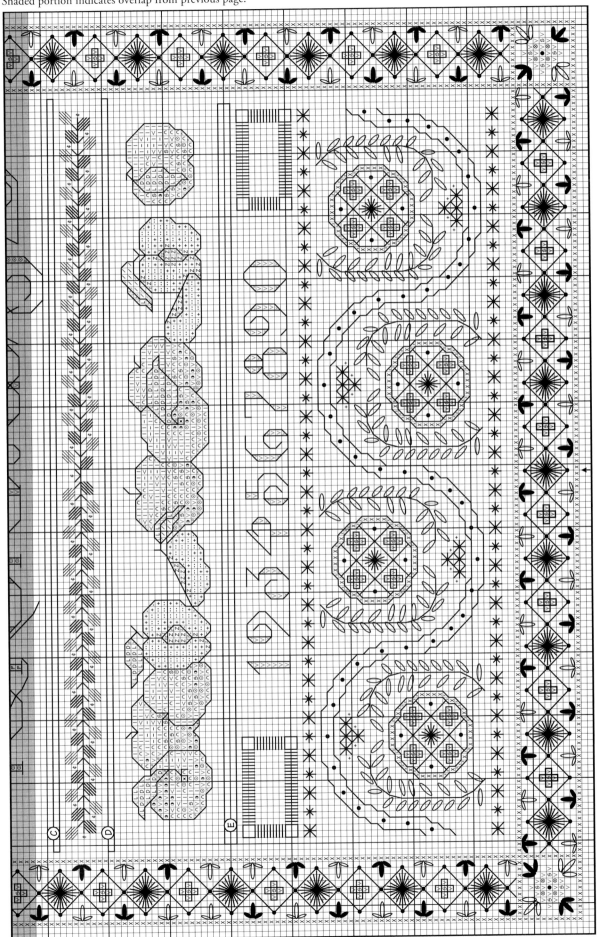

Peace Sampler

Designed with inspiration taken from eighteenth- and nineteenth-century samplers, this piece will be an eye-catching accent wherever it is displayed.

Inspired by samplers of the past, this simple design features an assortment of antique-sampler motifs and characteristics, including a strawberry border, a matched pair of birds, the ever-popular stag, and large trees that display the eighteenth-century fashion for topiary. The crown, a symbol of nobility, designates Jesus Christ as the Prince of Peace; and the stitched *peace* conveys a simple message of hope for the future.

Peace Sampler

DMC	Kreinik FT	Soie d'Alger		
• 500	2500	1846	blue green, vy. dk.	
X 501	2501	1844	blue green, dk.	
6 347	2327	2916	salmon, dk.	
○ 3328	2329	2915	salmon, med.	
∥ 677	2579	2534	old gold, vy. lt.	
v 676	2673	2243	old gold, lt.	
▲ 839	2839	4115	beige-brown, dk.	
3 927	2927	1744	gray-green, med.	
✳ 926	2926	1745	gray-green, dk.	

Fabric: 27-count unbleached linen from Norden Crafts
Stitch count: 125H x 155W
Design size:

27-count	9¼" x 11½"
30-count	8⅜" x 10⅜"
32-count	7⅞" x 9¾"
36-count	7" x 8⅝"

Instructions: Cross stitch over two threads, using two strands of floss unless otherwise indicated.
Special instructions:
Area 1: Work four-sided stitch for inner border, using two strands of floss.

Area 2: Work satin stitch in center of flower motifs, using two strands 677/2579/2534 and stitching in direction indicated by lines on chart.
Area 3: Work eyelet stitch using two strands of floss.
Area 4: Cross stitch over one thread, using one strand of floss.
Area 5: Work rice stitch over four threads, using two strands 500/2500/1846 for bottom cross and two strands 501/2501/1844 for top cross.
Area 6: Cross stitch over one thread, using one strand of floss.

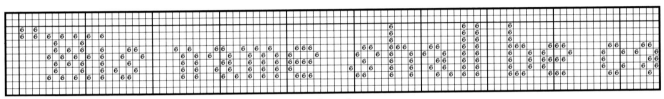

Area 6

Shaded portion indicates overlap from chart above.

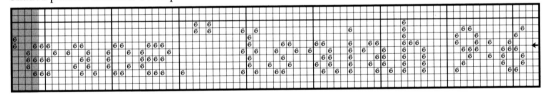

Shaded portion indicates overlap from chart above.

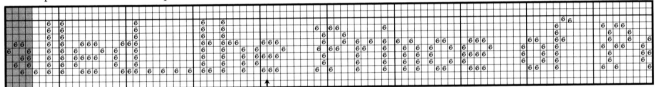

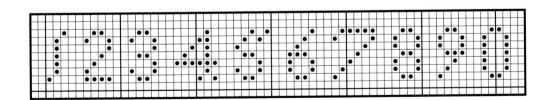

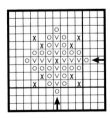

Area 4

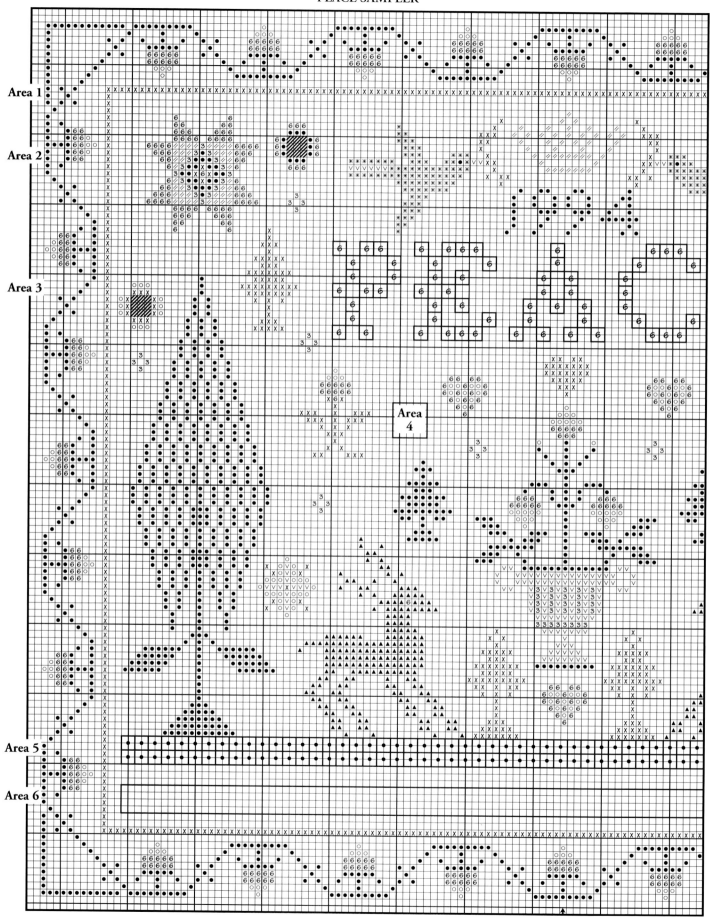

Area 1

Area 2

Area 3

Area 4

Area 5

Area 6

Shaded portion indicates overlap from previous page.

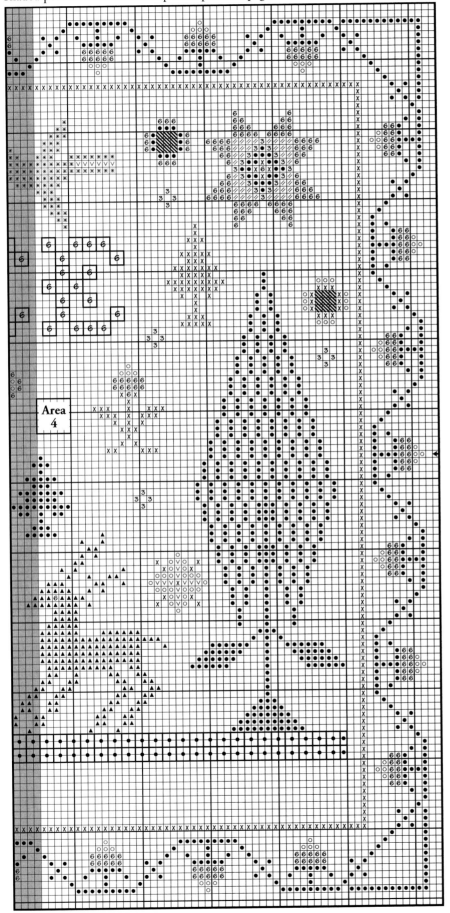

Area 4

Eyelet Stitch

Rice Stitch

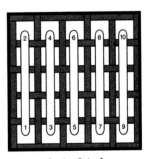

Satin Stitch

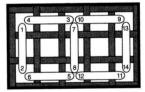

Four-Sided Stitch

Embroidered Purse

Antique Embroidered Purse

A reproduction of an antique piece from a private collection, this superb example of delicate embroidery will add the perfect finishing touch to a complementary evening ensemble and will also make an ideal carrying case for the little necessities belonging to a bride or her mother on that all-important wedding day. Enjoy testing your embroidery skills or learning new ones as you ply the stitches to create this exquisite accessory piece, which will be a lovely addition to the needleart enthusiast's collection of fine things.

Purse Back

NOTE: Perimeter lines are seam lines.
Seam allowance is not included on patterns.

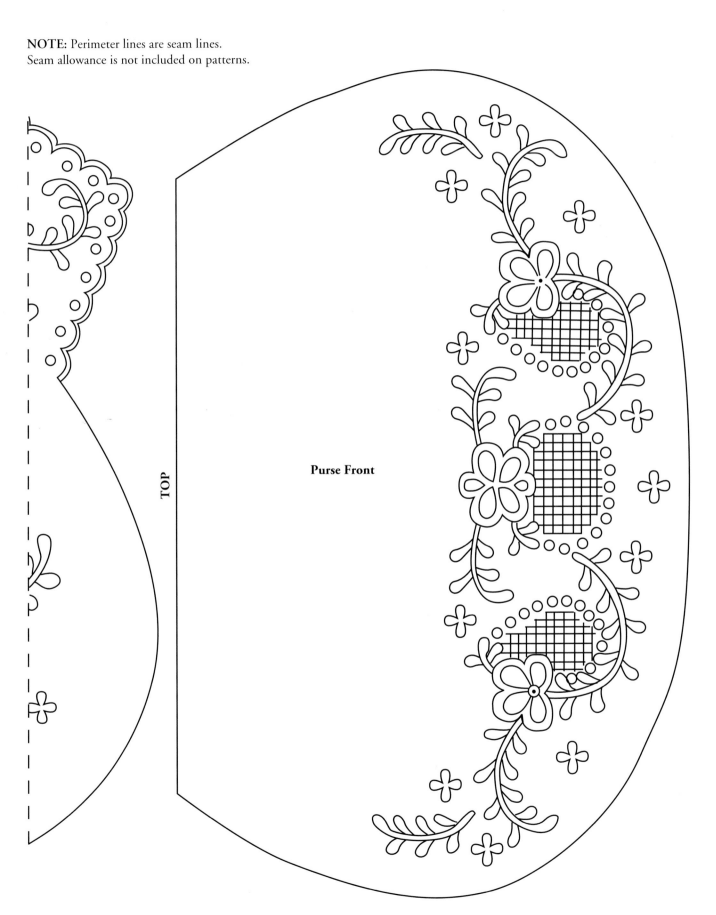

TOP

Purse Front

Embroidered Purse

Kreinik
Soie   DMC
d'Alger DMC FT
F2   ecru ecru ecru (three skeins)

Fabric: 50-count ivory Kingston linen from Zweigart®
Design size:
Purse front   3½" x 8"
Purse back & front flap 8¾" x 8¼"

Materials:
½ yd. 71"-wide Kingston linen from Zweigart®, color: ivory #222
½ yd. stiff sew-in interfacing
½ yd. 44/45"-wide ivory fabric (for lining)
1¾ yds. ⅜"-wide ivory satin ribbon, single- or double-face (for handle)
Fine-line mechanical pencil (for marking)
Large sewing scissors
Small, sharp, embroidery scissors
Ivory sewing thread
Hand-sewing needles
Straight pins
Measuring tape
1 small pearl button
Sewing machine
Iron

NOTE: Use a ½" seam allowance throughout.
1. Transfer all markings for embroidery to linen, using fine-line pencil, centering design, and leaving ample room for cut size of purse. Use a light touch when marking.
NOTE: Linen is fine enough that pattern will show through for tracing when it is placed underneath linen.
2. Work satin stitch for all flowers, stems, leaves, and dots, using two strands of silk.

Backstitch gridded areas using one strand of silk. Work buttonhole stitch around scalloped edge of front flap, using two strands of silk.
3. Press linen carefully from wrong side. Place linen pieces atop pattern pieces and trace cutting lines for purse. **Do not cut out.** Place linen pieces right-side up atop interfacing. Pin in place, being careful to keep grain of linen straight. Baste purse pieces to interfacing just inside cutting lines, using needle and one strand of sewing thread. For scalloped, front flap of purse, use basting stitches that can be removed easily along line of buttonhole stitches. Trim interfacing just inside indentations of scallops, trimming from wrong side of fabric. Cut out purse and interfacing pieces along cutting lines. For scallops along front edge of purse, use small, sharp, embroidery scissors to carefully cut linen next to buttonhole stitches, being careful not to cut stitches.
4. Cut two 3" x 11½" strips of linen. Seam together along short ends to make a long strip. Press seam open. Cut one 3" x 22" piece of interfacing. Baste linen band to interfacing, placing linen band right-side up and basting ⅜" from edge.
NOTE: This piece will form bottom and sides of purse.
5. Place the three pieces of the purse atop lining fabric and use purse pieces as patterns to mark cutting lines for lining. Trim edges of lining pieces ⅛" smaller all around than purse pieces. For lining along front, scalloped edge of purse, cut lining fabric even with outer edge of scallops.
6. Make a ¼"-long cut into edge of linen band approximately every ⅝", using embroidery scissors. Mark center of band and match to center of purse back, placing right sides of fabric together. Pin in place along edge of purse back and hand

baste layers together ⅜" from cut edge. Machine sew in place. Match opposite side of band to purse front, placing right sides of fabric together. Hand baste and then machine stitch. Clip seam allowances along curve and turn right-side out. Press seam allowances toward purse.
NOTE: A small towel, folded to size, can be placed inside purse and used as an ironing pad.
7. Repeat Step 6 to assemble lining pieces.
8. Sew pearl button in place at center of flower on purse front. Make a loop for button at center point of purse flap, hiding beginning and ending knots in interfacing. Set aside.
9. Cut satin ribbon into three equal lengths. Stack ribbon lengths together and sew across ribbon 1" from end. Secure sewn end of ribbon atop a flat surface and braid ribbon until braid is approximately 13" long. Sew across end to secure. Set aside.
10. Place lining inside purse, matching seams of purse and lining. Fold purse front under ½" and "finger press" edges. Fold down excess of band to meet top of purse front and back. Sew ribbon braid to band at each side for handle, hiding raw ends inside lining. Fold edge of lining under and pin to inside of purse. Hand sew in place.
11. From inside, take one "invisible" stitch at each side of purse, going through all layers at seam line and back into lining. (These stitches will secure lining to purse.)
12. Fold under edge of lining that meets purse flap. (**NOTE:** Lining should cover interfacing without sticking out from behind scallops.) Carefully hand sew in place, taking tiny, "invisible" stitches at indentation of each scallop to secure lining. Sew a small pleat in lining at back corners, if necessary. Remove basting along front flap.

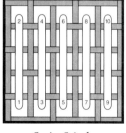

Satin Stitch

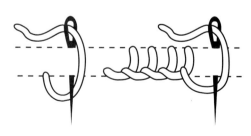

Buttonhole Stitch

Heart Sampler

This enchanting sampler design shows the understated elegance of white on white, combined with an assortment of stitches and techniques that will challenge the enthusiastic samplermaker of today. In addition to including a host of added stitches, this piece also contains cutwork and hemstitching. Glass beads add the finishing, decorative touches. Completed with complementary matting and a background that allows the detail and beauty of the stitchery to show, this design will make a splendid addition to a growing sampler collection or will make a wonderful gift. While not designed as a marriage sampler, the hearts make this piece ideal for such use. Simply substitute the initials of the couple for your initials and the date in the boxes on either side of the large, central heart.

A variety of stitches and techniques, including Hardangersøm and cutwork, were used to create this inspiring Heart Sampler.

Area A

Area C

Area E

Area F

Area B

Area B

Area D

Shaded portion indicates overlap from previous page.

Area G
Area H
Area I
Area J
Area K
Area L
Area M

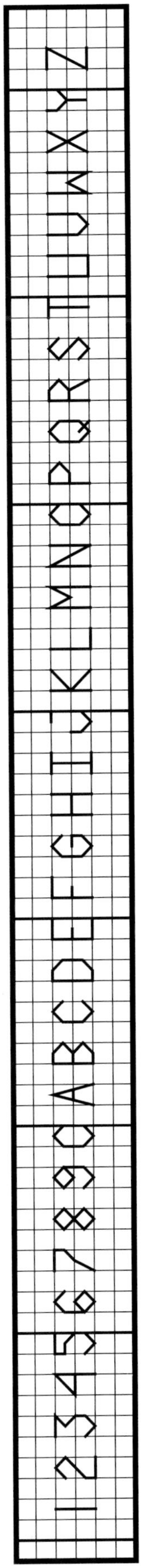

Heart Sampler

DMC	Kreinik FT	Soie d'Alger	
X	504	2504	122	blue green, lt.
△	746	ecru	2541	off white
○	762	2415	1732	pearl gray, vy. lt.
	225	2225	1011	pink, vy. lt.
	white	white blanc	white	

DMC Pearl Cotton (Coton Perlé)
#12 white
#8 white

Mill Hill Seed Beads
- 00479 white

Fabric: 25-count antique white Lugana from Zweigart®
Stitch count: 118H x 88W
Design size:

25-count	9½" x 7"
28-count	8½" x 6¼"
32-count	7⅜" x 5½"
36-count	6½" x 4⅞"

Instructions: Cross stitch over two threads, using two strands of floss. Backstitch using one strand of floss unless otherwise indicated.
NOTE: If a larger or smaller count fabric is used, the sizes of pearl cotton must be adjusted accordingly.

Special instructions: Please read all instructions before beginning. For best results, complete stitching in order listed.
Outer border
1. Work cross stitch.
2. Work satin stitch using DMC #8 pearl cotton.
3. Work eyelet stitch in corners, using DMC #12 pearl cotton.
4. Backstitch using one strand 225/2225/1011.

Corner motifs
1. Work satin stitch using DMC #8 pearl cotton.
2. Work cross stitch.
3. Work spider's web in center of square, using two strands 225/2225/1011.
Knotted cluster border
1. Hemstitch long edges of areas, using DMC #12 pearl cotton.
2. **Very carefully** cut the ten threads that run lengthwise in these areas, cutting very close to the satin-stitch bars of the corner motifs. Remove lengthwise threads, being careful not to pull fabric out of shape.
3. Using DMC #12 pearl cotton, draw every three clusters (six threads) together, referring to illustration on page 104 and anchoring floss at each end.
Area A
1. Work four-sided stitch using DMC #12 pearl cotton.
2. Work cross stitch.
3. Work satin stitch using DMC #8 pearl cotton.
4. Backstitch using one strand 762/2415/1732.
5. Work queen stitches using two strands white/white/blanc.
Area B
Work long-armed cross stitch using DMC #12 pearl cotton.
Area C
1. Work cross stitch.
2. Backstitch leaves using two strands 504/2504/122.
3. Work eyelet stitch near leaves, using two strands 225/2225/1011.
4. Work diamond eyelet stitch in center of medallions, using two strands white/white/blanc.
5. Work satin stitch using DMC #8 pearl cotton.
6. Backstitch using one strand 762/2415/1732.
Area D
Work herringbone stitch using DMC #12 pearl cotton.

Area E
1. Work diamond eyelet stitch over six threads, using two strands white/white/blanc.
2. Backstitch diamond eyelet stitch using one strand 762/2415/1732.
3. Work straight stitches between eyelet stitches, using DMC #8 pearl cotton.
Area F
1. Work eyelet-stitch variation using two strands white/white/blanc.
2. Work cross stitch.
3. Work kloster blocks (perpendicular) using DMC #8 pearl cotton.
4. Work eyelet stitch using DMC #12 pearl cotton.
5. **Very carefully** cut threads where small dots appear, cutting very close to the satin-stitch bars. Remove threads, being careful not to pull fabric out of shape.
6. Needleweave remaining threads using DMC #12 pearl cotton, inserting dove's eyes where indicated on chart.
Area G
1. Work Smyrna cross stitch using two strands 504/2504/122.
2. Work rice stitch where large boxes appear, using DMC #8 pearl cotton for legs 1–2 and 3–4, and one strand white/white/blanc for remaining legs.
Area H
Work Montenegrin cross stitch using DMC #12 pearl cotton.
Area I
1. Work cross stitch.
2. Work diagonal satin stitch using DMC #8 pearl cotton.
3. Work satin stitch for hearts, using two strands 225/2225/1011 for the first heart and alternating with two strands 762/2415/1732 to finish the row.
Area J
1. Work satin-stitch bar at each end of row, using DMC #8 pearl cotton.
2. **Very carefully** cut the central six horizontal threads between the satin-stitch bars,

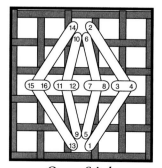

Queen Stitch

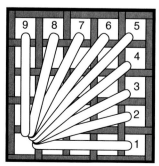

Eyelet-Stitch Variation

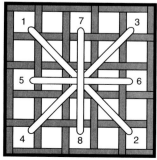

Smyrna Cross Stitch

Rice Stitch

cutting very close to the bars. Remove threads, being careful not to pull fabric out of shape.

3. Hemstitch between the bars, using DMC #12 pearl cotton.

NOTE: Catch four threads per cluster in the top row of hemstitching. In the bottom row, catch two threads in the first cluster, four threads across the row, and then two threads in the last cluster. This gives the trellis effect.

Area K

Work horizontal knitting stitch using two strands white/white/blanc.

Area L (initial and date blocks)

1. Work satin stitch using DMC #8 pearl cotton.

2. Work Smyrna cross stitch in corners, using DMC #12 pearl cotton.

3. Backstitch initials and year in blocks, using two strands 504/2504/122 and alphabet and numerals provided.

Area M (large heart)

1. Work cross stitch.

2. Work straight stitch for net pattern, using DMC #12 pearl cotton. Be careful not to pull fabric out of shape. Stitch lines going from top left to bottom right first; then stitch lines going from top right to bottom left, weaving over and under the stitches already in place.

3. Work small, upright cross stitches using two strands 504/2504/122.

4. Backstitch around heart, using one strand 504/2504/122 for inner line and one strand 225/2225/1011 for outer line.

Bead placement

Attach beads where symbol • appears, using one strand white/white/blanc.

Spider's Web

Work a foundation of an odd number of spokes, using evenly spaced straight stitches radiating from a center point. Beginning in center, weave a second thread over and under the spokes, working outward from the center and being careful not to catch fabric ground. Secure thread on back side of fabric.

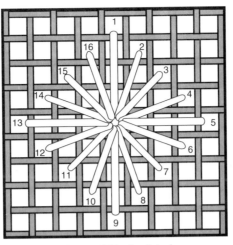

Diamond Eyelet Stitch

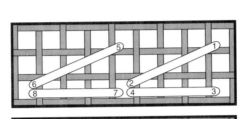

Hemstitch 4 x 2 (Area J)

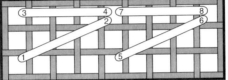

Satin Stitch

Eyelet Stitch

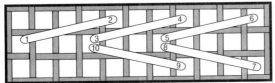

Horizontal Knitting Stitch

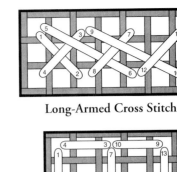

Long-Armed Cross Stitch

Four-Sided Stitch

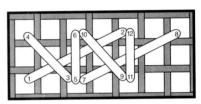

Montenegrin Cross Stitch

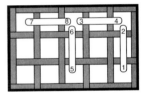

Hemstitch 2 x 2
(knotted cluster border)

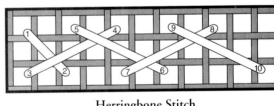

Herringbone Stitch

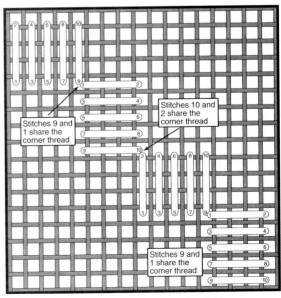

Stitches 9 and 1 share the corner thread

Stitches 10 and 2 share the corner thread

Stitches 9 and 1 share the corner thread

Kloster Blocks (Perpendicular)

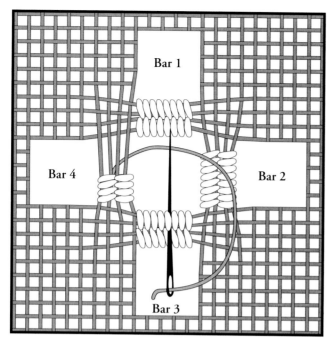

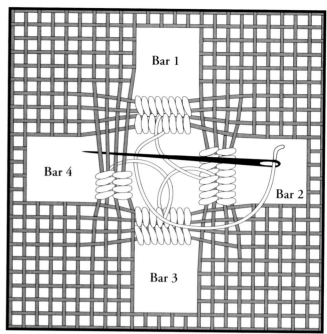

Dove's Eye

Needleweaving/Dove's Eye

To begin needleweaving, use an away waste knot, placing knot in fabric above bar that is to be woven. Begin weaving over the first two fabric threads and under the last two (Figure 1). Continue weaving over two and under two until bar is full, using tight tension and working in a figure-eight motion (Figure 2). Finish bar with thread toward next bar to be woven. Begin next bar by going over two fabric threads and under two fabric threads (Figure 3). Con-

tinue needleweaving to center of bar four. From this point, go down with needle in center of bar three to begin Dove's Eye. Bring needle over the thread going from bar four to bar three, and go down in center of bar two. Bring needle over the thread going from bar three to bar two and go down in center of bar one. Bring needle over the thread going from bar two to bar one. Bring needle under the thread from bar four to bar three and go down in center of bar four. Finish needleweaving bar four. Cut away waste knot and weave thread tail under stitches on back side of work.

NOTE: If bars are woven in a clockwise direction, the dove's-eye is worked counterclockwise. When the dove's-eye is worked next to a kloster block, treat the block as a bar by

going down in the center stitch, splitting the thread.

Knotted Clusters

Draw every three clusters together with a knot by passing needle behind clusters and bringing it out through loop. Pull tight and repeat to end of border.

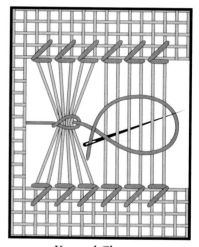

Knotted Clusters

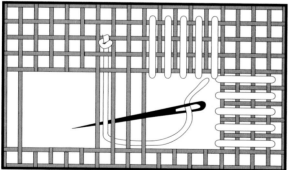

Needleweaving—Fig. 1

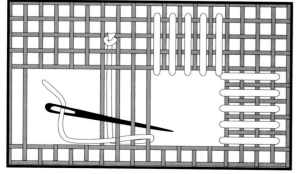

Needleweaving—Fig. 2

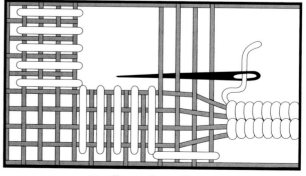

Needleweaving—Fig. 3

Christmas Sampler

Although this Christmas Sampler *contains motifs that make it particularly appropriate for display during the holiday season, its timeless message and the use of muted floss shades that stray from traditional, seasonal colors make it a decorative delight that can also be displayed throughout the year.*

A meandering, strawberry border surrounds this inspiring sampler design, which includes a stitched depiction of the manger scene in Bethlehem. Created to mark the birth of Christ and to herald the Christmas season,

this piece will bring joy both while it is being stitched and while it is used to decorate the home. Complete this everlasting treasure for yourself or present it to a loved one or a very special friend.

Area 1

Area 2

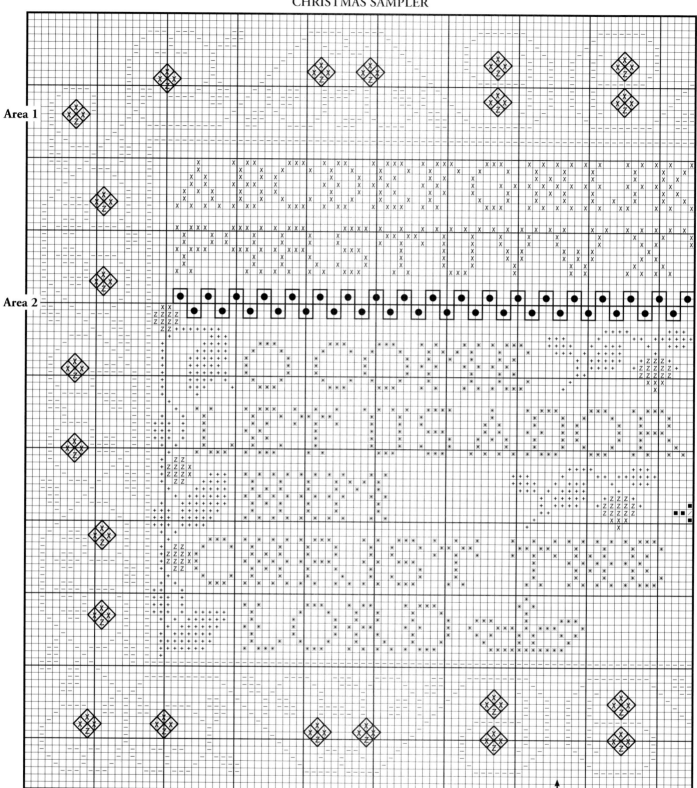

Area 3

Christmas Sampler

	DMC	Kreinik		
	DMC	FT	Soie d'Alger	
X	356	2356	4612	terra cotta, med.
+	522	—	1832	fern green
•	927	2927	1814	gray-green, med.
✱	3740	—	—	antique violet, dk.
■	370	2831	2214	mustard, med.
○	3768	2768	1745	gray-green, dk.
◢	318	2318	1743	steel gray, lt.
/	372	2579	3833	mustard, lt.
−	520	—	1835	fern green, dk.
Z	758	2758	643	terra cotta, lt.

Fabric: 27-count cream linen from Norden Crafts
Stitch count: 103H x 148W
Design size:

25-count	8¼" x 11⅞"	
27-count	7⅝" x 11"	
30-count	6⅞" x 9⅞"	
32-count	6½" x 9¼"	

Instructions: Cross stitch over two threads, using two strands of floss. Straight stitch using two strands of floss.

Special instructions:

Area 1: Work queen stitch for strawberries, using two strands of floss.

Area 2: Work eyelet stitch using two strands of floss.

Area 3: Work diamond eyelet stitch for star, using two strands of floss.

Eyelet Stitch

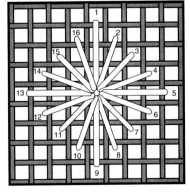

Diamond Eyelet Stitch

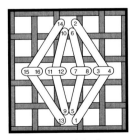

Queen Stitch

Hearts and Flowers Accessories

Delicate hearts and flowers are the focal point of this wonderful, five-piece accessories set. Created especially to hold the needle mavin's assortment of stitching implements, this quintet of lovely repositories will occupy many pleasurable hours as you ply the stitches to create each piece. If you have a collection of small, antique buttons, take the designer's lead and use them to embellish the inside of the needlecase. The buttons shown came from her mother's collection. The phrase stitched on the inside of the needlecase was taken from a sampler design worked by the designer more than a decade ago. The verse in its entirety reads as follows:

Needle small with magic pow'r
Charmer of the circling hour
May thy various uses be
Ever understood by me

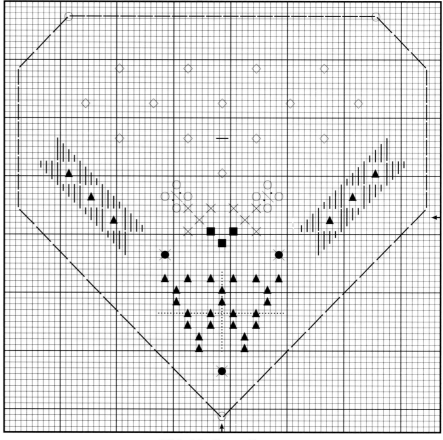

Thimble Case—Front

Hearts and Flowers Accessories

Note: For these projects, a general list of materials has been given. Specific materials for each project have been listed separately.

General materials:

#24 tapestry needle	Scissors
Measuring tape	Iron

	DMC	Kreinik		
	DMC	FT	Soie d'Alger	
◇	3689	2574	1041	mauve, lt.
▲	3688	2572	1042	mauve, med.
■	3687	2570	3024	mauve
✖	676	2833	2611	old gold, lt.
○	932	2932	1713	antique blue, lt.
✕	3363	2469	1843	pine green, med.

DMC #8 Pearl Cotton (Coton Perlé)
932 antique blue, lt.

Linen Thread
35/2 soft white
50/2 soft white

Fabric: 30-count soft white linen
Thimble Case
(**NOTE:** Cut one 4" square for *Front* and one 5" square for *Back*.)
Scissors Case
(**NOTE:** Cut two 7" squares.)
Needlecase
(**NOTE:** Cut three 6" squares.)
Pin Holder
(**NOTE:** Cut two 8" squares.)

Workbox
(**NOTE:** Cut one 12" square.)

Design size:
Thimble Case
Front
30-count 2⅓" x 2½"
Back
30-count 3⅛" x 2½"
Scissors Case
30-count 3¼" x 2⅜"
Needlecase
Front
30-count 3⅜" x 3⅝"
Back & Inside
30-count 3¾" x 3¾"
Pin Holder
30-count 2¾" square (3¾" diagonal measure)
Workbox
30-count 6⅞" x 6⅞"

NOTE: Please read instructions carefully before beginning. Grid lines on charts represent weave of linen. Broken lines on charts indicate placement of chain-stitch outlines.

Chain Stitch

Instructions:
Center chain-stitch outline on linen squares. Work chain stitch over three threads, using one strand pearl cotton. Work four-sided stitch over **three** threads, working each stitch twice and using one strand 50/2 linen thread. **NOTE:** Designer worked four-sided stitches vertically, rather than horizontally, and worked the stitches so as to pull the thread toward herself. Using this method results in more-consistent tension when pulling the thread, and lends a nicer-looking finished appearance to the project. Cross stitch over two threads, using two strands of floss unless otherwise indicated. Work satin stitch using two strands 3689/2574/1041. Center initial in area marked by large, dotted +, using alphabet provided. Work Smyrna cross stitch

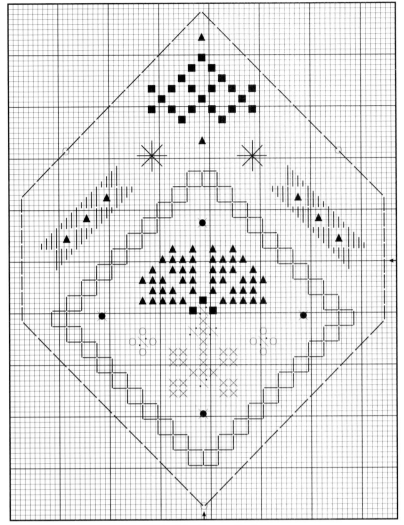

Thimble Case—Back

where large ✳ appears, using one strand 35/2 linen thread. Work Palestrina stitch where ✕ appears, using one strand 35/2 linen thread.

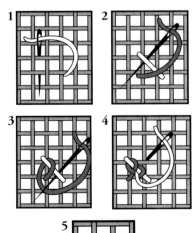

Palestrina Stitch

Special instructions:

Thimble Case: Four-sided stitch placement is eight threads from bottom tip of chain-stitch outline.

Scissors Case & Needlecase: Four-sided stitch placement is eight threads from bottom tip of chain-stitch outline. For cross stitches over one thread, use one strand of floss.

Pin Holder: Four-sided stitch placement is twelve threads from bottom tip of chain-stitch outline. For cross stitches over one thread, use one strand of floss.

Workbox: Corner chain stitches located in first outline are over four threads. For cross stitches over one thread, use one strand of floss.

Finishing instructions:
Thimble Case
Materials:
One 4" square and one 5" square light pink silk fabric

One 4" square and one 5" square light weight fusible interlining

One 4" square and one 5" square ⅛"-thick lightweight fleece

12" length 4mm-wide pink silk ribbon

3" length gold elastic cord

⅛" pearl button   #7 sharp needle

1. Complete stitching following instructions given.

2. Press each side face-down atop soft cloth.

3. Sew on button where indicated by — on chart for front, using two strands 3687/2570/3024 and sewing over two vertical threads.

4. Trim seam allowances to ½" from chain-stitch outline.

5. Use stitched and trimmed front and back as templates for cutting one silk lining for each side.

6. Fold seam allowances along chain-stitch outline as follows. For front, fold tip first and miter point; then fold the diagonal sides, the vertical sides, and the top. For back, fold tips first and miter points, then fold sides.

7. Use each folded side as a template to cut one piece fleece and one piece interlining for each side.

8. Sew elastic-cord loop at tip of back side.

9. Unfold seam allowances of sides and place fleece pieces inside. Fold seam allowances back over batting.

10. Center interlining atop wrong side of silk fabric for each side. Fuse interlining to silk. Fold seam allowances of silk as for

111

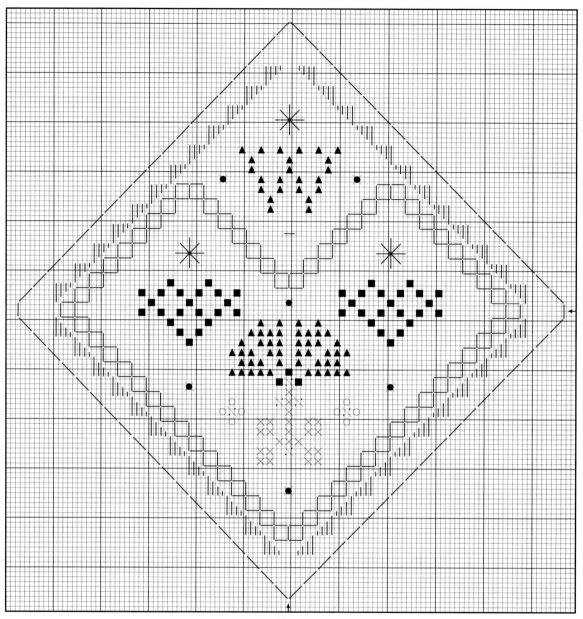

Pin Holder—Front

seam allowances of stitched front and back. Place wrong side of front silk lining to wrong side of front stitched design. Repeat for back pieces.

NOTE: Fleece will be under seam allowances of stitched-design side.

11. Sew silk lining to each side, using small slip stitches and one strand 3689/2574/1041. Share same "hole" of each chain stitch to guide length of slip stitch.

12. Hold front and back sides together, placing silk linings together and matching chain stitches. Join sides together with a half cross stitch, using one strand pearl cotton and inserting needle under the two "inside loops." To join front and back, begin with an away waste knot and work a locking loop stitch, beginning at bottom

heart tip, continuing on each side, and stopping at large circles as indicated on chart. Use same locking stitch to end joining, rethread at away waste knot, and end tail of thread between lining and fleece.

13. To make pillow to place at bottom heart tip, cut a 1" square from fleece and a 1¼" square from silk. Cover fleece square with silk and fold diagonally. Fold seam allowances of silk to inside of triangle and slip stitch closed, using one strand 3689/2574/1041. Place pillow inside heart-shaped case at bottom tip and secure by piercing tiny pillow as you insert needle between lining and fleece, taking two stitches, and then ending thread inside case.

14. Thread #24 needle with 6"-length silk ribbon and insert needle at left or right

112

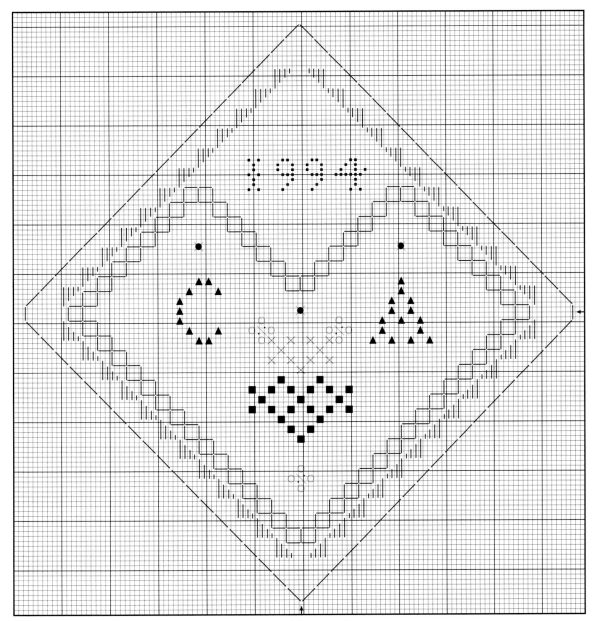

Pin Holder—Back

side of bottom tip of heart between front and back sides. Bring ribbon out opposite side, remove needle, and tie a small bow. Turn case over and repeat. Trim ribbon tails to desired length.

Pin Holder
Materials:
Three 5" squares ⅛"-thick lightweight fusible fleece
Two 5" squares white lightweight mat **or** cardboard
18" length 4mm-wide pink silk ribbon
⅛" pearl button

1. Follow steps 1–4 for *Thimble Case*, trimming all seam allowances to ¾" from chain-stitch outline.

2. Fold seam allowances along chain-stitch outline. Miter points first, then fold diagonal sides.

3. Use one folded, pin-holder side as a template to cut two cardboard squares approximately ⅛" smaller than chain-stitch outline. Trim off point of cardboard at each corner. Use folded pin-holder template to cut three fleece squares. Trim one fleece square to match size of cardboard squares.

4. Unfold seam allowances of pin-holder sides and place fleece pieces fusible-side down inside chain-stitch outline. Press to fuse to wrong sides of stitched front and back of pin holder.

5. Place cardboard squares inside seam allowances of pin holder on front and back sides. Center remaining fleece piece on

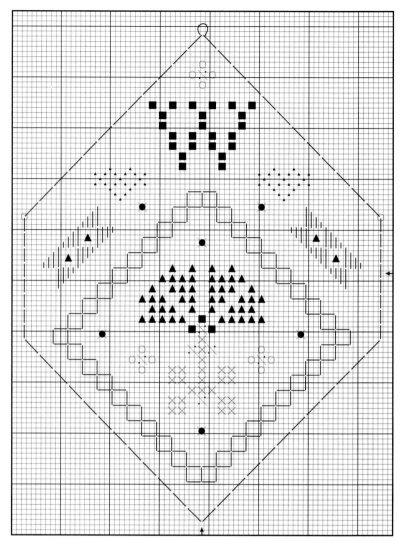

Scissors Case—Front

cardboard of front pin holder. Fold seam allowances back over on front and back sides of pin holder.

6. Hold front and back sides of pin holder together, noting top and bottom of design on each side, with fleece of front side facing cardboard of back side. Match chain-stitch outlines.

7. Join sides together with a half cross stitch, using one strand pearl cotton and inserting needle under the two "inside loops." To begin, leave a 4" tail of thread and start with a locking loop stitch on left side at bottom point. Continue up left side and stop at top point with a locking loop stitch, leaving a 4" tail. Repeat for right side. Tie thread tails together at top and bottom, rethread needle, and end threads inside pin holder between the two sides.

8. Follow step 14 for *Thimble Case*. With remaining length of ribbon, tie one small bow at top. Store pins by inserting at edge between front and back sides of pin holder.

Scissors Case
Materials:
Two 5" squares light pink silk fabric
Two 5" squares lightweight fusible inter
    facing
Two 5" squares ⅛"-thick, lightweight fus
    ible fleece
12" length 4mm-wide pink silk ribbon
3" length gold elastic cord
⅛" pearl button   #7 sharp needle

1. Follow steps 1–2 for *Thimble Case*.
2. Sew on button where indicated by — on chart for front of *Scissors Case*, using two strands 3687/2570/3024 and sewing

over two threads at inside border of center chain stitches.
NOTE: Button is placed between silk lining and linen back and "sits" above chain stitches when *Scissors Case* is closed.
3. Follow steps 4–5 for *Thimble Case*.
4. Fold seam allowances along chain-stitch outline as follows. For front, fold tips first and miter points. Then fold diagonal sides, and then vertical sides. For back, fold tip first and miter point; then fold diagonal sides, vertical sides, and top.
5. Use each folded side as a template to cut one piece batting and one piece interfacing for each side.
6. Follow step 8 for *Thimble Case*.
7. Unfold seam allowances of sides and place fleece pieces inside. Fuse to wrong side of stitched linen. Fold seam allowances back over fleece.
8. Follow step 10 for *Thimble Case*, using interfacing.
9. Follow step 11 for *Thimble Case*.

10. Follow step 12 for *Thimble Case*, ending tail of thread between lining and linen.
11. Follow step 14 for *Thimble Case*.

Workbox
Materials:
6½" x 3¼"-tall box (**NOTE:** Designer
    used workbox from Home Arts.)
8" square ¼"-thick fusible fleece
8" square lightweight fusible interfacing
16" length 4mm-wide pink silk ribbon
Two ⅛" pearl buttons

1. Follow steps 1–3 for *Thimble Case*.
2. Center interfacing atop wrong side of linen box lid and fuse lightly with iron.
3. Trim seam allowances to 2" from chain-stitch outline.
4. Identify box-lid foundation from workbox. Use lid foundation as a template to cut one square of ¼"-thick fleece. Fuse fleece to wrong side of interfaced, linen box lid.

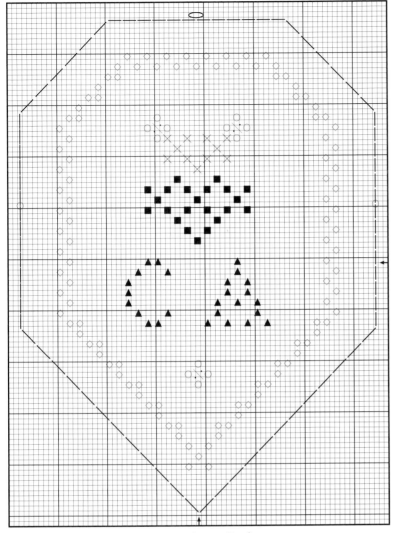

Scissors Case—Back

NOTE: If using a thinner fleece, add layers until chain-stitch outline is located at edge of box-lid foundation when linen box lid is wrapped over it.

Constructing the box:
Materials:

Stitched, prepared linen box lid

½ yd. 44/45"-wide mauve moiré fabric, cut into two 8" squares and two 4" x 28" strips

8" square light pink silk fabric

Three 8" squares ¼"-thick fleece

60" length blue-and-gold cord trim

Tacky glue

Thin-bodied tacky glue (**NOTE:** Add small amount of water to tacky glue.)

1" foam **or** regular paintbrush

Pinch-type clothespins   Sandpaper

Large rubber band   Heavy book

NOTE: Lightly sand any "bumps" on edges of foundation.

Identify cut-fabric and box-foundation pieces:

Stitched and prepared linen box lid (for lid)

Two 8"-square mauve moiré fabric pieces (for inner lid and base)

8" square light pink silk fabric (for inner base)

Two 4" x 28" strips mauve moiré fabric (for band and band liners)

Construct lid and base:

NOTE: The two largest foundation squares are the lid and the base. The two second-largest foundation squares are the inner lid and the inner base.

1. Spread thin, even amount of thin-bodied tacky glue on one side of lid foundation, using paintbrush. Set glue-side down atop wrong (fleece) side of prepared, linen box lid. Place dab of tacky glue on each corner of foundation and spread with brush. Pull corners of linen box lid over foundation corners

and into glue until chain-stitch outline is located at edges of box-lid foundation. Spread a small amount of glue around remaining edges of foundation. Pull linen over all edges, mitering corners. Let dry.

2. For inner lid, spread thin amount thin-bodied tacky glue on inner-lid foundation. Center lid glue-side down atop 8" square of fleece. Smooth and let dry, then trim fleece even with foundation. On wrong side of foundation, spread glue on each corner and wrap mauve moiré fabric over foundation. Then spread glue around remaining edges and pull fabric over edges, mitering corners. Set heavy book atop inner lid and let dry.

3. Join inner lid to lid by spreading tacky glue on wrong side of inner lid. Then place inner lid and lid with wrong sides together, centering inner lid to lid and leaving a lip around outside edge. Secure with clothespins and let dry.

4. For inner base, spread thin-bodied glue over inner-base foundation, center over 8" square fleece and let dry. Trim fleece to outside edge of inner base. Place fleece-side down atop wrong side of silk fabric and put dab of tacky glue at each corner of base. Pull fabric over base at corners; then spread small amount of glue around remaining edges of base foundation and pull fabric over all edges, mitering corners. Place heavy book on top of base, covering fabric to protect while drying. Repeat for base, using 8" square of mauve moiré fabric and fleece. Spread wrong side of inner-base foundation with tacky glue and center over wrong side of base foundation. Place heavy book atop base, remembering to protect fabric. Let dry.

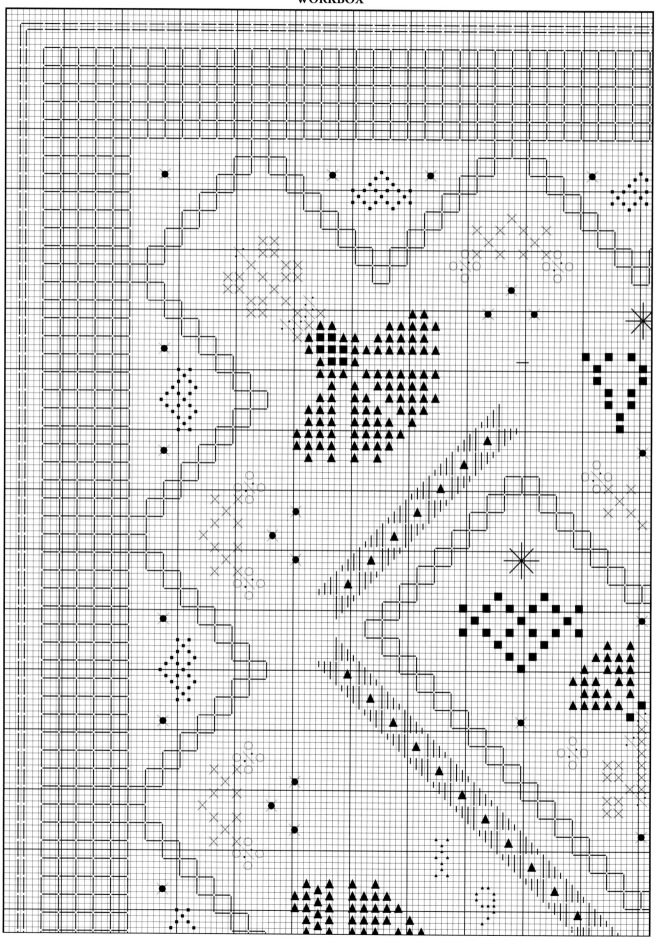

Shaded portion indicates overlap from previous page.

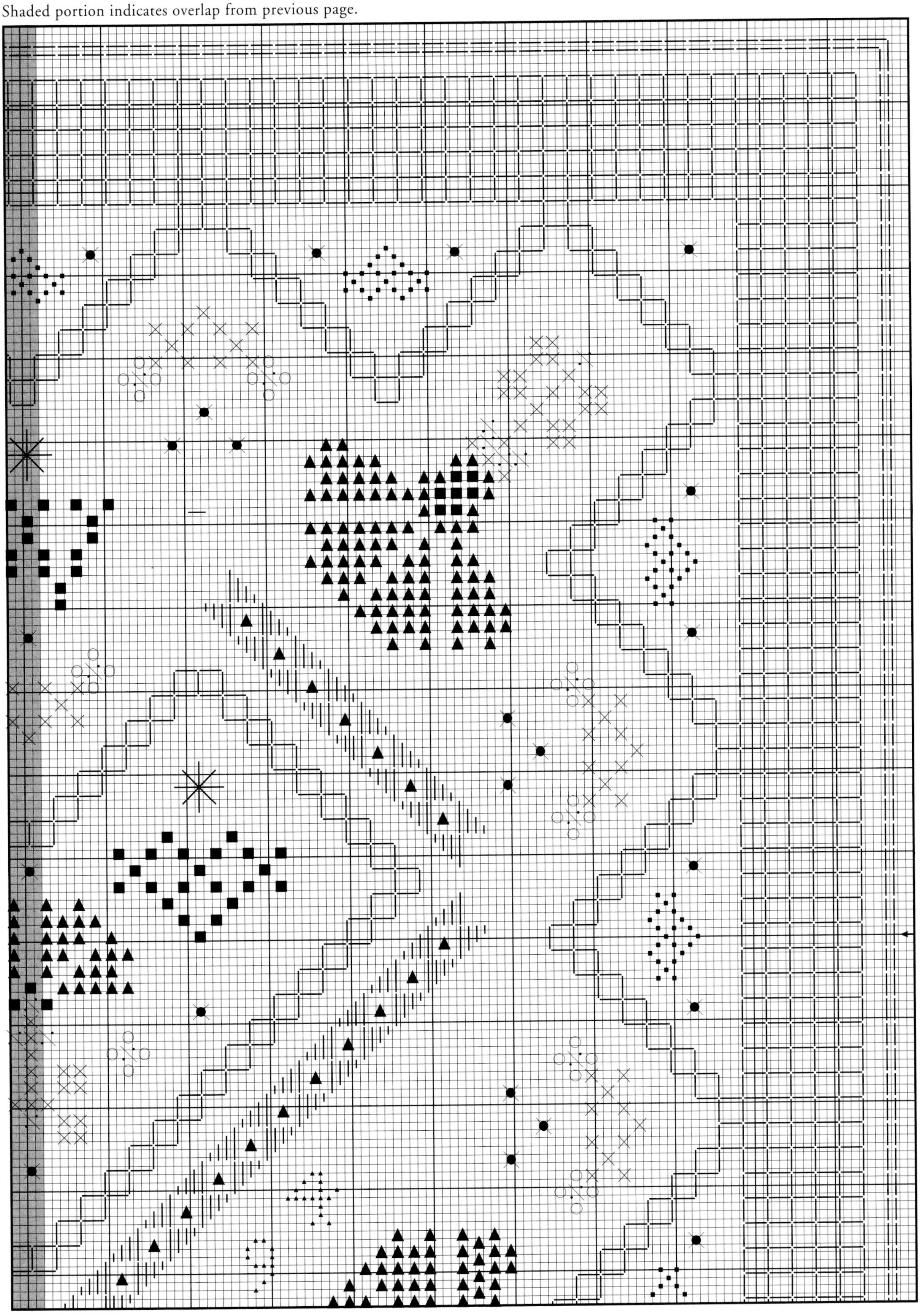

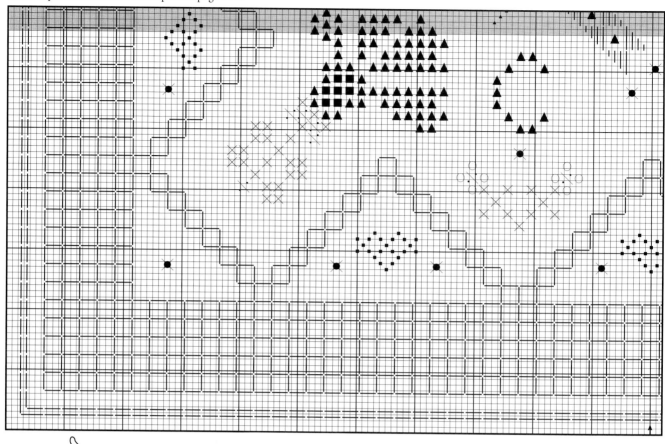

Locking Loop Stitch
NOTE: The Locking Loop Stitch is a joining stitch that does not pierce the fabric but simply "laces" the chain stitches together.

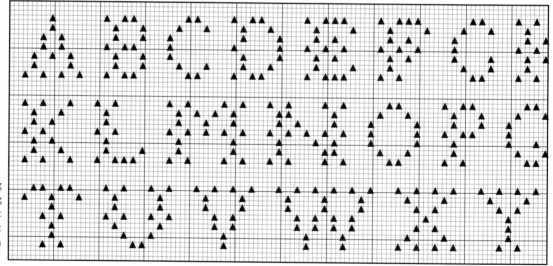

Construct bands:

NOTE: Four widest foundation strips are bands. They form outside edges of box. Four narrower strips are band liners. They will be placed on inside of box.

1. Form outside band first. Draw a pencil line ¾" up from long edge of fabric strip, drawing line on wrong side of fabric. This line will be guide for keeping band-foundation pieces straight. Spread thin, even amount thin-bodied glue on one side of band foundation and place atop fabric strip, placing along pencil line and leaving ½" of fabric extending from end. Refer to Workbox Bands Illustration. As you place each band-foundation piece, turn over and smooth fabric. Glue all four band-foundation pieces on strip of fabric, leaving exactly ⅛" space between each band-foundation piece. Cut fabric strip ½" from end of last band-foundation piece. Turn fabric over the two ends and glue down. Spread glue along long edges and fold fabric over into glue, forming band strip. Form band frame by bending band strip between band foundations so that one edge of band butts against side of adjacent band. Continue bending band strip between each band, allowing only one edge of each band to butt. (**NOTE:** Corners must be at right angles to fit properly.) Use tacky glue to glue end pieces together. Hold band frame in place with large rubber band. Let dry.

2. Run line of tacky glue along outside lip of inner base. Place bottom of band frame over edges of inner base, aligning all sides. Place heavy book on top and wipe away any excess glue around lip. Let dry.

118

Shaded portion indicates overlap from previous page and page 117.

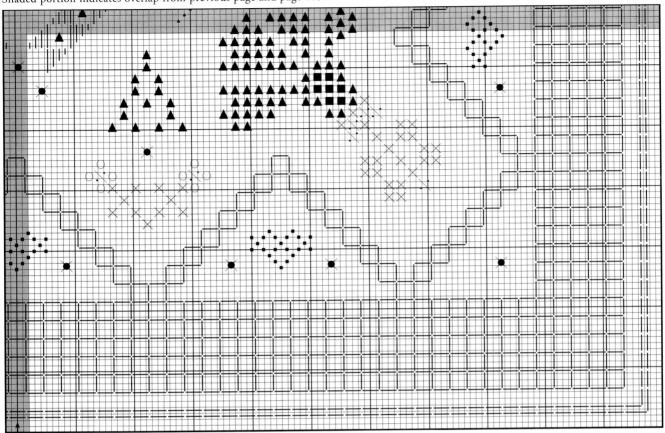

Shaded portion indicates overlap from previous page.

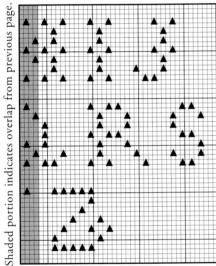

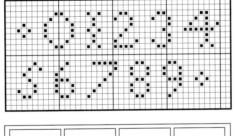

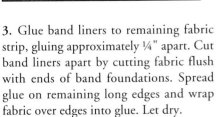

Workbox Bands Illustration

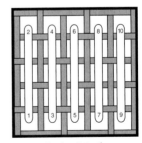

Four-Sided Stitch (worked vertically)

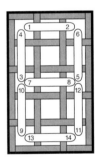

Satin Stitch

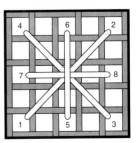

**Smyrna Cross Stitch
(worked from left to right)**

3. Glue band liners to remaining fabric strip, gluing approximately ¼" apart. Cut band liners apart by cutting fabric flush with ends of band foundations. Spread glue on remaining long edges and wrap fabric over edges into glue. Let dry. **NOTE:** Fabric does not cover each end of band liners. Note that two of these band liners are shorter than the others.

4. Place band liners inside box bottom, resting upon inner base and leaving a lip around top edge of box. Assemble as follows: spread glue on wrong side of one long

119

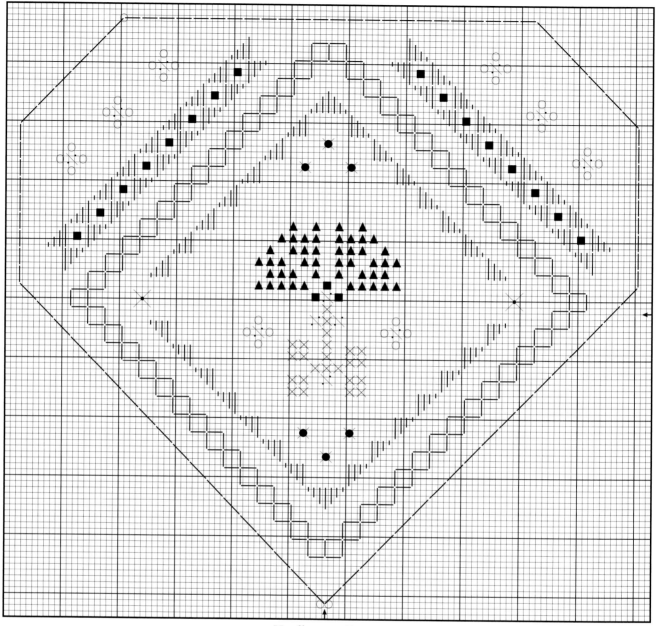

Needlecase—Front

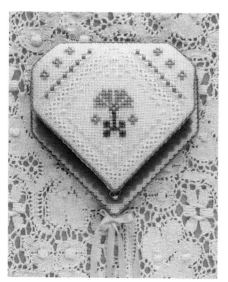

band liner and place on inside of band. Repeat, placing second long band liner directly across from first. Shorter band liners go in last, butting against longer band liners. Place lid on box, turn over atop a thick towel, and place heavy book on top. Let dry.

5. Place blue-and-gold cording around outside lip of lid along edge of inner base, applying thin line of tacky glue and pressing cording into ditch. Cut ends carefully, seal with small amount of glue, and butt ends together. Repeat application of cording around outside of band frame on base of box.

6. Cut 16" length of silk ribbon in half. Thread #24 needle with tip of one strand of silk ribbon and insert into four-sided stitch located at center of bottom border.

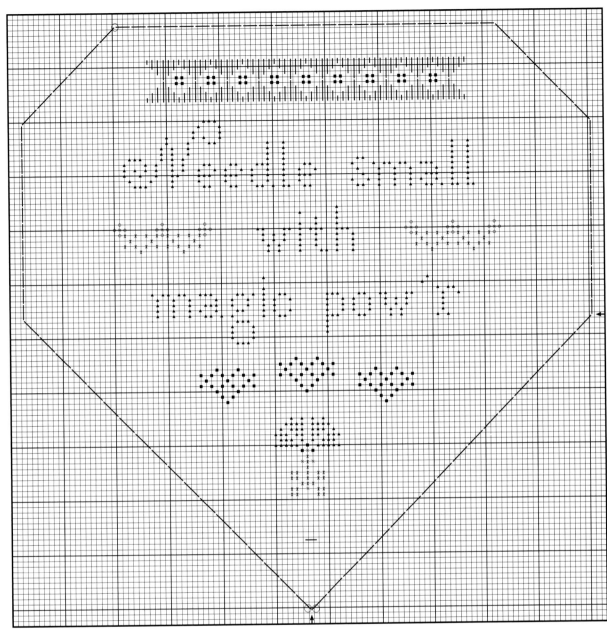

Needlecase—Center

Insert only into linen stitch, rather than into fused interfacing. Remove needle and draw silk ribbon through carefully. Tie a small bow. Repeat with remaining length of silk ribbon, using same four-sided stitch but tying bow below first bow. Trim ribbon tails to desired length.

Needlecase
Materials:
6" square pink silk fabric
6" square pink medium-weight felt
Four 6" squares lightweight fusible fleece
6" square white lightweight mat board
24" length 4mm-wide pink silk ribbon
3" length gold elastic cord   Pinking shears
Decorative buttons (optional)

1. Follow steps 1–4 for *Thimble Case.*
2. Use needlecase-front outline as a template for cutting two fleece interlinings. Cut one silk-fabric heart with ½" seam allowance beyond outline.
3. Using needlecase inside outline as a template, cut two fleece interlinings, one mat-board heart, and one felt heart.
4. Prepare bottom of needlecase by pressing fleece to wrong side of each design. Fold seam allowances along diagonal sides first, then along vertical sides. Fold top of heart last. Place mat-board heart inside seam allowances to check fit. Wrap top design ("Needle small. . .") tightly over mat board and glue lightly. Hold back design to opposite side of mat board and match

121

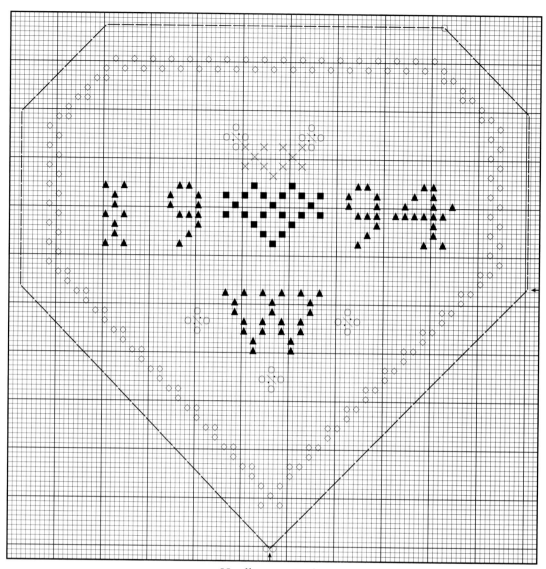

Needlecase—Back

chain stitches. Join hearts together with a half cross stitch, using one strand pearl cotton and inserting needle through the two "inside loops." Begin at bottom heart tip with a locking loop stitch and continue up each side, stopping at dot on chart. Use same locking stitch to end joining, rethread at away waste knot, and end tail of thread between layers of heart.

5. Trim felt-heart edges with pinking shears and center over bottom half of needlecase, leaving ¼" margin on all sides. Cut felt triangle pocket with pinking shears and place at bottom of heart for sizing. Sew decorative buttons to triangle if desired; then glue triangle at lower, outside edges with a thin line of tacky glue on felt heart. Cut a tiny buttonhole at tip of felt heart and button heart to bottom of needlecase.

6. Prepare top of needlecase by pressing fleece to wrong side of design. Fold seam allowances along chain-stitch outline. Sew

elastic-cord loop at heart tip. Place wrong side of silk fabric to non-fusible side of fleece and fold margins to fusible side. Press lightly.

7. Hold fleece sides together and slip stitch silk lining to design side, using one strand 3689/2574/1041. Share same "hole" of each chain stitch to guide length of slip stitch. Begin at heart tip and end tails at dot on chart.

8. Join top of needlecase to bottom by matching chain stitches at top of heart and weaving together, using pearl cotton. Begin with an away waste knot and work a locking loop stitch across top side of needlecase. Use locking stitch to end joining, rethread at away waste knot, and end tail of thread between lining and linen.

9. Follow step 14 for *Thimble Case*, using a 12" length of silk ribbon and inserting needle at left or right side of bottom tip of heart on bottom side of needlecase.

122

Trio of Hearts

A trio of designs makes up this assortment of stitchery. Fashioned to fit atop purchased, heart charms, these pieces can also be finished as small, sweet-smelling pomanders. Use them to scent fine wearables or as ornamental touches for curtain tiebacks.

Counted and pulled stitches and petit point, accented by beadwork, form this threesome of delightful, heart designs. Ideal accent pieces, these charmers provide a wonderful way to display needlework and have the added benefit of being quick-to-complete gifts.

Trio of Hearts

Note: For these projects, a general list of finishing materials has been given. Specific finishing materials for each project have been listed separately.

General materials:
#26 tapestry needle
3½" x 2" piece of cardboard
Disappearing-ink fabric-marking pen
Beading needle
White paper
Terry towel
Scissors
Iron

Butterfly Heart Sachet

DMC Kreinik

DMC	FT	Soie d'Alger	
ecru	ecru	F2	ecru
3782	2611	3412	mocha brown, lt.
3773	2407	2632	flesh, med.

Linen Thread
50/2 natural

Mill Hill Seed Beads
V 3021 Royal Pearl
○ 0275 Coral

Fabric: 28-count tea-dyed linen from Charles Craft, Inc. (**NOTE:** Cut two 6" squares.)
Stitch count: 22H x 27W
Design size:

28-count	1½" x 2"
30-count	1½" x 1¾"
32-count	1⅜" x 1¾"
36-count	1¼" x 1½"

Instructions: Work four-sided stitch variation as indicated on chart, using one strand linen thread and pulling with medium tension. Backstitch antennae using two strands 3773/2407/2632.

Finishing instructions:
Materials:
Two 5" squares lightweight fabric to match linen (for lining)
Potpourri
Sewing thread
Straight pins

1. Complete stitching following instructions given.

2. To block piece, soak in cold water for fifteen minutes. Wrap in terry towel to remove excess moisture. Use iron to press piece face-down atop dry towel.

3. Attach pearl beads using two strands ecru/ecru/F2. Attach coral beads using two strands 3773/2407/2632.

4. Cut heart shape from white paper, using Pattern B. Center atop stitched piece and trace around edge, using disappearing-ink fabric-marking pen. Cut out. Use this pattern to cut out linen backing and front and back lining pieces.

5. Sew lining pieces together, using a ½" seam allowance and leaving an opening for turning. Trim seams, clip corners, and turn.

6. Fill lining with potpourri. Turn raw edges of seams to inside and whipstitch opening closed.

7. Sew linen pieces together, placing right sides of fabric together and leaving an opening for turning. Trim seams, clip corners, and turn. Insert stuffed, lining heart. Turn raw edges of seams to inside and whipstitch opening closed.

8. Make cord, using a 100" length of 3782/2611/3412 and following instructions for making cording. Whipstitch cord to heart, using one strand 3782/2611/3412 and centering middle of cord at point of heart. Overlap cord at top center of heart and stitch through to secure. Tie a bow in remainder of cording. Tie a slip knot at desired length at each end of cording and unravel cording to knot.

9. Make and attach tassel, using 3773/2407/2632 and following instructions for making a tassel. Attach pearl beads using 3773/2407/2632.

Floral Heart Charm

DMC Kreinik

DMC	FT	Soie d'Alger	
712	ecru	creme	cream
738	2738	2621	tan, vy. lt.

DMC #8 Pearl Cotton (Coton Perlé)
712 cream (one ball)

Kreinik Blending Filament
002 gold

AK Designs Beads
○ 809 Size 11 gold
809 Bugle Bead gold

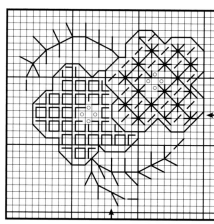

FLORAL HEART CHARM

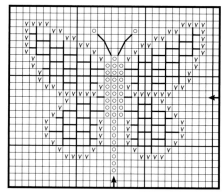

BUTTERFLY HEART SACHET

Linen Thread
50/2 Ivory

Fabric: 28-count cream linen from Charles Craft, Inc. (**NOTE:** Cut one 6" square.)

Stitch count: 27H x 27W
Design size:

28-count	2" x 2"
30-count	1⅞" x 1⅞"
32-count	1¾" x 1¾"
36-count	1½" x 1½"

Instructions: Work backstitch portion of whipped-backstitch outline of flowers, using one strand pearl cotton. Work Algerian eye stitches using one strand of linen thread and pulling each leg with medium tension. Backstitch between Algerian eye stitches, using one strand pearl cotton. Work four-sided stitch variation as indicated on chart, using one strand linen thread and pulling tightly. Whip the backstitch using one strand pearl cotton. Work stems in whipped backstitch, using a blend of one strand 738/2738/2621 and two strands blending filament.

Finishing instructions:
Materials:
Medium heart charm

1. Complete stitching following instructions given.

2. To block piece, soak in cold water for fifteen minutes. Wrap in terry towel to remove excess moisture. Use iron to press piece face-down atop dry towel.

3. Attach beads using two strands 738/2738/2621.

4. Using pattern provided with charm, cut out one heart shape from paper. Center atop stitched piece, and trace around edge, using disappearing-ink fabric-marking pen. Cut out.

5. Center stitched piece atop charm. Wrap fabric edges around charm edges and secure fabric edges in charm's teeth. **Do not** put back of charm on at this time.

6. Make cord using a 50" length of 712/ecru/creme, following instructions for making cording. Whipstitch cord to front edge of heart, using one strand 712/ecru/creme. Overlap ends of cord at top center of heart and bring to back.

7. Snap on back of charm.

8. Make corded hanger using a 60" length of 712/ecru/creme. Pass through charm clasp and knot with a slip knot 3" from clasp. Cut ends to 1" and unravel to knot.

9. Make and attach tassel, using 738/2738/2621 and following instructions for making a tassel. Wrap using two strands 738/2738/2621 blended with six strands blending filament. Add gold beads using 738/2738/2621.

Initialed Heart Charm

DMC	Kreinik FT	Soie d'Alger	
+ 307	2743	543	lemon
○ 899	2899	3013	rose, med.
╱ 932	2932	1713	antique blue, lt. (two skeins)
• 991	2958	1826	aqua, dk.
white	white	blanc	white (two skeins)

Linen Thread
40/2   cream

Strand Sheen
1   white

AK Designs Beads
2mm pearls

Fabric: 28-count white linen from Charles Craft, Inc. (**NOTE:** Cut one 6" square.)
Stitch count: 46H x 49W
Design size:

28-count	3¼" x 3½"
30-count	3" x 3¼"
32-count	2⅞" x 3"
36-count	2½" x 2¾"

Instructions: Work initial and flower in petit point, using two strands of floss. Work double rows of single faggot stitch, using one strand of linen thread and pulling with medium tension. Backstitch using three strands of Strand Sheen.

Finishing instructions:
Materials:
Medium heart charm
One 4" square thin fleece
One 4" square white fabric (for lining)

1. Complete stitching following instructions given.

2. To block piece, soak in cold water for fifteen minutes. Wrap in terry towel to remove excess moisture. Use iron to press piece face-down atop dry towel.

3. Attach pearls using two strands white/white/blanc.

4. Cut one heart shape **each** from fleece and lining fabric ⅛" larger around perimeter than Pattern A.

5. Using pattern provided with charm, cut out one heart shape from paper. Center atop stitched piece, trace around edge using disappearing-ink fabric-marking pen, and cut out.

6. Layer fleece, lining fabric right-side up, and stitched front right-side up atop charm, centering all pieces atop charm. Wrap fabric edges around charm edges and secure fabric edges in charm's teeth. **Do not** put back of charm on at this time.

7. Make cord using a 50" length of white/white/blanc, following instructions for making cording. Whipstitch cord to front edge of heart, using one strand white/white/blanc. Overlap ends of cord at top center of heart and bring to back.

8. Snap on back of charm.

9. Make corded hanger using a 60" length of white/white/blanc. Pass through charm clasp and knot with a slip knot 3" from clasp. Cut ends to 1" and unravel to knot.

10. Make and attach tassel, using 932/2932/1713 and following instructions for making a tassel. Attach pearls to tassel, using two strands 932/2932/1713.

Instructions for making a tassel:
Cut one 8" and one 12" length of floss from a complete skein, keeping all six strands together. Wrap remainder of skein around cardboard twenty-five times and cut away leftover floss. Insert 8" length under top of wrapped thread and tie firmly. Cut the bottom loops of floss. Bring 12" length of floss up through center of tassel and wrap tightly six times. Thread end through needle and whipstitch wraps, leaving a small space between stitches. Pass needle through center of tassel and cut thread end to match tassel ends. To attach tassel to ornament,

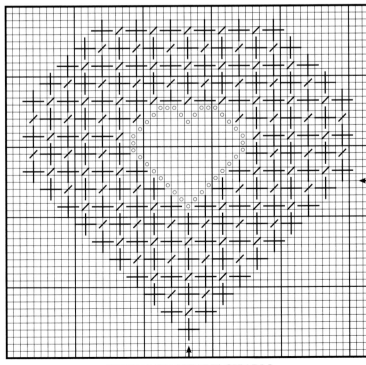

INITIALED HEART CHARM

loosen top knot. Thread one end through needle and pass through fabric behind cord at heart point. Retie knot and hide knot inside tassel. Run ends through center. Trim ends of tassel to make them even.

How-tos for making ornament cording:
To make cording trim, cut length of floss indicated from skein. Bring raw ends of floss together, dividing length in half. Tie a knot in floss end with raw edges. Insert fingers through center of looped end and move wrist in a circular motion to twist, continuing until floss tightens around fingers. Remove fingers without letting go of twist. Hand-twist remaining portion. Bring the two ends together, holding securely and dividing in the middle with one finger. Remove finger from middle dividing point, letting floss twist. Run hand over length of floss several times to smooth. Tie a knot in raw-edge end to hold twist.

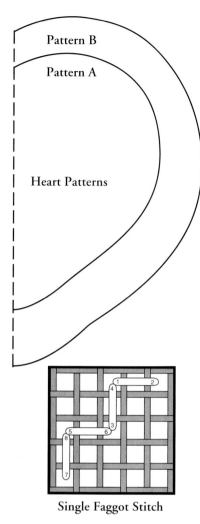

Pattern B

Pattern A

Heart Patterns

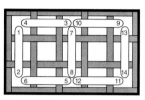

Four-Sided Stitch

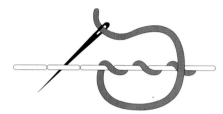

Whipped Backstitch

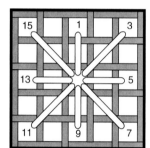

Algerian Eye Stitch

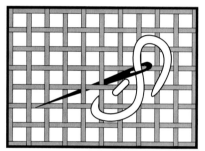

Petit Point

Single Faggot Stitch

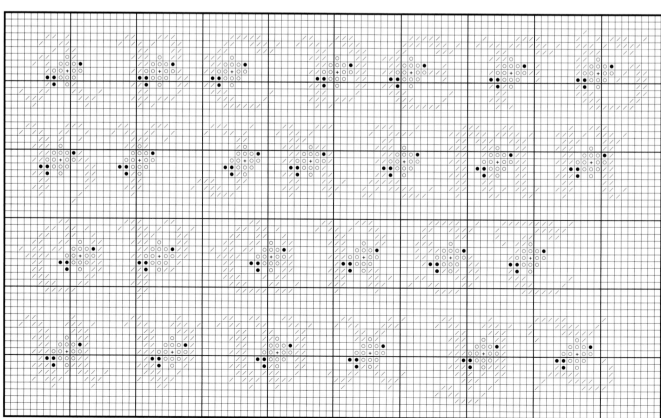

126

Shaker-Box Samplers

This threesome of coordinating pieces was designed to fit atop a pair of Shaker boxes and a matching pincushion. Created with an eye for the colors so popular for today's interior decorating, these appealing pieces will add charm to the needlewoman's nook while providing functional storage space for her handiworking supplies.

The clean, simple lines of Shaker-inspired boxes form the perfect foundation for this trio of designs.

Area 1

Area 2

Area 3

Large

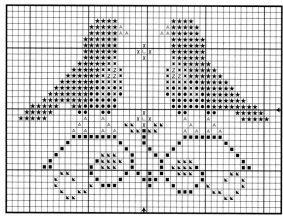

Area 2

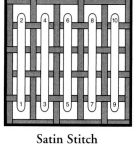

Satin Stitch

Eyelet Stitch

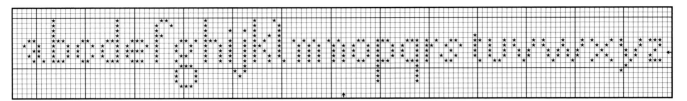

Area 3

Shaker-Box Samplers

	DMC	FT	DMC Kreinik Soie d'Alger	
•ǀ•	502	2502	1843	blue green
X	931	2931	1714	antique blue, med.
★	3750	2929	1716	antique blue, vy. dk.
∧	729	2783	2242	old gold, med.
L	676	2673	2243	old gold, lt.
╱	3047	2579	2231	yellow-beige, lt.
Z	760	2760	2932	salmon
✗	3712	2329	2915	salmon, med.
•	347	2327	2916	salmon, dk.
☒	367	2320	1835	pistachio, dk.
■	890	2890	1846	pistachio, ul. dk.

Fabric: 32-count dirty linen Belfast linen from Zweigart®

Stitch count:

Small	46H x 43W
Medium	62H x 59W
Large	100H x 97W

Design size:

Small

18-count	2½" x 2⅜"
25-count	3¾" x 3½"
28-count	3¼" x 3"
32-count	2⅞" x 2¾"

Medium

18-count	3½" x 3¼"
25-count	5" x 4¾"
28-count	4½" x 4¼"
32-count	3⅞" x 3¾"

Large

18-count	5½" x 5⅜"
25-count	8" x 7¾"
28-count	7⅛" x 7"
32-count	6¼" x 6"

Instructions: Cross stitch over two threads, using two strands of floss. Work satin stitch using two strands 3047/2579/2231, stitching in direction indicated by lines on chart. Personalize using sampler alphabet and numerals.

Special instructions:

Large Sampler

Area 1: Work eyelet stitch using two strands of floss.

Areas 2 & 3: Cross stitch over one thread, using one strand of floss.

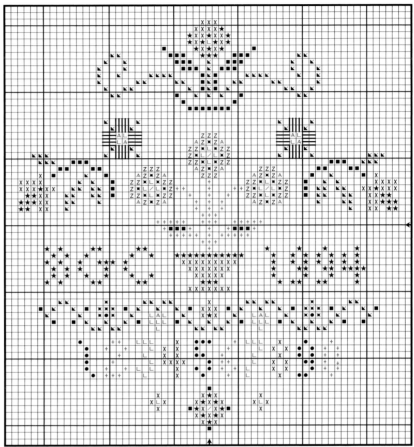

Medium

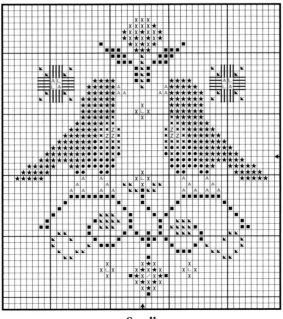

Small

A Glossary for Collectors of Needlework Tools

(Above) 1) Avery brass butterfly, Victorian, holds two needle packets under each wing, English, c. 1871; 2) Avery brass walnut, Victorian, holds needles inside nut, English, c. 1873. Photos show both pieces closed (top) and open (bottom).

The entire vocabulary of the Industrial Revolution would not suffice to identify or explain the products and processes to which it gave birth. In the field of needlework tools, many predate that era of explosive production, including the not-so-humble needle and the finger-defending thimble. The glossary that follows is intended for the collector of those needlework tools used for handwork, although that, in itself, is a nebulous area of concentration. Certainly cutting out a dress pattern is a part of handwork, and a sock stretcher was very useful to our grandmothers in drying handknitted socks. Should those items be included, and others of like categories, this would be a project for a doctoral dissertation. The subsequent list of terms is therefore brief and, undoubtedly there will be words that some feel were unjustifiably omitted. Basically, three areas are covered in this effort: materials, tools, and identifying terms, including manufacturers of interest and styles of design. It is the hope of every researcher that the information

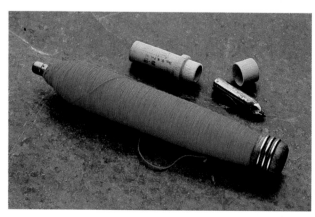

(Above) Machine bobbins: 1) Boye brand sewing-machine bobbin in wooden case, American, c. 1906; 2) Wooden machine bobbin, used in textile mills through the 1970s, American.

presented will encourage others to delve more deeply into a particular area of interest, increasing and sharing new knowledge with those of like passion.

abalone—The thin lining of nacre from the inside of the abalone mollusk, often darker and more colorful than mother-of-pearl but equally iridescent.

agate—A variegated form of quartz in a rainbow of colors, used atop thimbles and for the handles of handwork tools such as tambour hooks.

aide-mémoire—Several small, thin sheets of ivory upon which notes might be written, suspended from a chatelaine and usually protected by a covering of the same material from which the chatelaine was made.

Aix-la-Chapelle—German city known for the manufacture of needles.

aluminum—A soft, blue-white base metal often used for promotional and advertising gimmicks such as thimbles. It is too soft to hold the cutting edge of scissors but strong enough to use in crochet hooks and knitting needles.

Art Deco—An early-twentieth-century design style incorporating smooth and geometric elements, including borders, alphabets, and figures.

art needle—One of several sized needles inserted in a handle to form loops on the right side of fabric by entering through the reverse side.

Art Nouveau—A turn-of-the-century design style incorporating exceptionally fluid lines, often portraying figures with ephemeral qualities.

Avery—William Avery and Son of Redditch, England, designed the most-prized brass needlecases of the late-nineteenth century. Most are ingenious in the manner in which they hold needle packets (i.e. under butterfly wings, in the canvas of an artist's easel). Stamped with a British Registry mark, they are easily dated. The majority also have the name stamped: W. Avery & Son.

Bakelite®—A synthetic resin and forerunner of plastic from which tools have been made. Similar to hard rubber, it is durable and easily colored.

beadwork—Any manner in which beads are attached or incorporated in the composition or design of a needlework tool. They may be sewn on a pincushion, added as decoration on a needlebook, threaded on wire and wrapped around a needlecase or other implement container.

beech wood—A hardwood tree of the same family as the oak or chestnut, typical background wood used in the construction of Tunbridgeware tools.

beeswax—Used in thread waxers to strengthen thread or to keep it from tangling.

Berlin work—Designs worked from colored patterns designed on graph paper. Much like the charted designs for modern cross stitch or needlepoint, they were used in the early and middle-nineteenth century by makers of Tunbridgeware and for beadwork designs.

birch—A close-grained hardwood tree used for mosaic work in Tunbridge designs.

bobbins—Any of a number of tools upon which thread or yarn is wound to be used while needlework is in progress, unlike a threadwinder or spool from which thread is cut in varying lengths to accommodate a project.

bodkin—Usually a flattened, needle-shaped tool used for threading and lacing ribbon or cord directly through fabric and casings. Often one end was sharp while the other had an elongated eye to accommodate the lacing material. Some bodkins had a slit at one end and a large, round eye at the opposite end for cord and ribbon and were identified as ribbon threaders. Bodkins were usually included in fitted sewing boxes.

bodkin cases—Flat cases with friction closures to hold bodkins.

bog wood—Sometimes called bog oak. Any wood taken from a peat bog where it hardened and blackened over time. Usually decoratively carved into tools, especially the bases for pincushions.

bone—Any part of the skeletal system of an animal except for teeth or tusks, which were considered to be ivory. The mate-

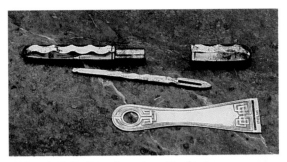

(Above) 1) Bodkin, faceted steel in friction-closure case, English, c. 1860; 2) Ribbon threader, sterling silver, one of a graduated set, "flat" eye for ribbon; round eye for cord, Art deco, American, c. 1900.

(Above) Cotton barrel, sterling, monogrammed "EC," American, c. 1900.

(Left) Steel and brass chatelaine with nautical motif. Accessories include scissors sheath, thimble holder, aide-de-mémoire, and tape measure. Scissors not original. English, c. 1860.

rial from which almost every conceivable tool might be made, it is distinguished from ivory by the porous striations that may be seen by looking at the tool from the end of the piece.

brass—An alloy consisting of copper and zinc, it is a yellow color, highly workable, and used for most needlework tools. It is relatively inexpensive and therefore popular for quotidian tools in whole or in part.

Bristol board—The forerunner of modern perforated paper, it was a fine paste board with no glazing on either side. It was worked like modern perforated paper and often incorporated into needlebook covers or tops of boxes.

bronze—An alloy chiefly of copper and tin and one of the earliest materials used in the production of needles and thimbles.

button—A flat or knob-shaped item sewn to a garment for the purpose of fastening or closing it. The button is

passed through a hole on a second part of the garment to secure the two parts.

button remover—A flat-bladed tool with a V-shaped cut in one end that is honed to a sharp enough edge that, when slipped under a secured button, it will cut the thread.

buttonhole cutter—A flat-bladed, V-shaped tool that cut the holes for buttons to pass through. It was usually covered by a sheath upon which measurements were noted to gauge the size of the hole.

buttonhole gauge—A small tool with a sliding gauge that measured the size of a button so that the buttonhole size would be of the proper proportion to the button.

calyx-eyed—A needle with a tiny cut through the top of the eye, through which the thread was pulled downward into the eye.

cartouche—An oval or oblong design usually surrounded by decorative border.

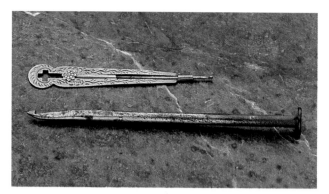

(Top) Crochet hooks: 1) Brass and steel, with retractable hook, c. 1870;
2) Primitive, fashioned from steel nail, American. (Above left) Darning eggs:
1) Sterling silver and wood, probably English for the American market, c. 1870;
2) Bakelite®, handle holds needles, English, c. 1930. (Above right) 1) Tomato
emery, silk, red with simple yellow plaid, felt top, probably English;
2) Strawberry emery, silk faille with fine felt top, probably American,
early twentieth century.

A monogram is often engraved inside the border on fine tools, especially on those of precious metals.

celluloid—A polymer created in the mid-nineteenth century that closely resembles ivory in color. Genuine celluloid items in good condition may cost as much or more than some silver and gold tools.

ceramic—Baked clay that may be glazed, painted, and otherwise decorated. Because it is easily broken, old tools are rare.

chase—The ornamentation of a metal surface by embossing or engraving.

chatelaine—Any of a number of cases or clasps attached at the waist of clothing from which tools were suspended on varying lengths of chain to include scissors, aide-mémoires, needlecases, thimble containers, magnifying glasses, etc. Separate items from chatelaines are often found in the marketplace, but a complete chatelaine with all of the original pieces is rare and costly.

chinoiserie—That which is Chinese or which imitates an oriental style or design.

cloisonné—A surface decoration where enamel is partitioned by metal wire or by a raised pattern.

Coats & Clark—Separately or combined, the name(s) of thread companies that actively provided advertising articles for the needleworker, as well as manufactured and sold tools and containers that bear their logo(s). Both commercial and private items are very collectible, including the small boxes in which the thread was sold.

commemorative—That which is crafted to memorialize a special event, whether joyous or sad.

copper—A malleable, reddish-colored, common metal.

coquilla nut—An egg-shaped nutshell from which thread containers and thimble holders were carved or turned. Often confused with the corozo nut.

cork—The tissue of a cork oak. Used for tool handles, to line tool containers, and occasionally as cushion to make friction closures tighter.

corozo nut—Also called vegetable ivory or mutton ivory, it is the nut of a Colombian palm tree from which a variety of small tools were carved or turned, particularly during the eighteenth century.

cotton barrel—A thread container that enclosed a small spool upon which thread was wound. Sometimes the spool extended through the top of the barrel for winding. A tiny hole, through which thread was drawn for use, was drilled in the barrel.

crochet hook—A hooked tool with a handle for crocheting. Available in sizes suitable for working with all weights of thread and yarn. Sometimes called a shepherd's hook.

darner—Usually an egg or mushroom shape at the end of a handle, the tool was used for mending socks and gloves by pulling the worn or torn area over the smooth surface for ease of darning. Often the handle unscrewed to serve as a needle container.

disc—Disc pincushions, emeries, and waxers are made by confining between two discs of the same material and size the necessary filling to serve the intended purpose. Matched pieces are usually found in fitted workboxes. Disc pincushions are still made in limited quantities today.

D.M.C.—Dollfus-Mieg & Cie (known to today's needlework enthusiasts as The DMC Corporation). A French company, established in 1746, that is a manufacturer of thread and yarn that is distributed worldwide. The company also purveys a variety of tools and books of patterns, including the famous *The Encyclopedia of Needlework* by Thérèse

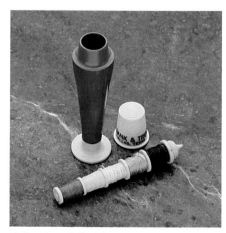

(Above) Celluloid hussif, advertising
"Texas Bank and Trust Co.," holds
needlecase/thread winder, American, c.1930.

(Above left) Knitting needles: *1) All wood, the green knobs are for easy size identification, Susan Bates Co., American; 2) Black-tipped celluloid, English, 1920–1940.* *(Above right)* Lace bobbins: *1) Ivory, inscribed "Jesus Wept," English, 1840–1900; 2) Wood, probably pine, machine-turned, English, 1840–1900.*

de Dillmont. Early editions of the book are highly collectible.

Dorcas—Among thimble collectors, a prized item is the Dorcas thimble, which was produced with a steel core to add strength and was patented in 1884.

ebonized wood—A black lacquer used on wood and other surfaces to give the appearance of ebony.

ebony—A tree, or the wood thereof, which is exceptionally hard. That which is black holds a high gloss when polished and is the most prized.

electroplate—Any process by which an object is coated, especially metal items, by means of electrolysis.

ell—An old unit of measure equaling about forty-five inches. Sometimes found on very old measuring tapes and sticks.

emboss—Any process by which the surface of an item is raised, usually to form a decorative motif.

emery—A tool often resembling a small pincushion, which holds some form of polishing powder. Pins and needles were thrust through the powder to remove rust and rough places.

enamel—A composition, usually opaque, used to coat the surface of an object for decorative or protective purposes.

engrave—To incise a design or lettering, especially in metals, with a hard tool. Sometimes used in regard to woodworking, but then the word *carve* is usually used.

etch—The production of a design on metal or glass, using a corrosive substance.

etui—A small, fitted tool box holding items for personal care and/or needlework. Sometimes referred to as a nécessaire, it is differentiated from a lady's companion by the items it contains. The former holds personal-care items, while the latter holds only needlework and writing tools. Produced during the eighteenth and nineteenth centuries, a complete box is rare.

fernware—Originally the process of decorating an item by varnishing bits of live fern on the surface. Later, printed paper with fern motifs was used.

figural—A term referring to a tool, meaning that it resembles, particularly a person, but sometimes an animal. Rarely, it means any recognizable object as opposed to one that is fashioned simply to serve a purpose.

finger guard—Worn like a thimble, for protection, on the left forefinger of the left hand. The top of the guard is cut out to accommodate the tip and inside of the finger only.

forge—The basic process of heating and working metal by use of a furnace. A forge is also the location where the process takes place.

glass—An amorphous substance usually made by fusing silicates. Fragile because of its brittleness, few old tools have survived and new tools are usually made as decorative and/or commemorative and souvenir pieces.

gold—A yellow-colored, very precious metal, heavy in weight. Used for tools and the fittings of cases and containers. Seldom used for scissor blades but not uncommon for scissor handles and bows. Gold tools have always been costly and are not widely available to collectors. According to the metals with which gold is mixed, gold may be considered green, white, or pink, in addition to yellow.

gold-filled—Defined differently in different time periods. At one time equated with gold plating, it may also mean an alloy of gold with a base metal where the percentage of gold is minimal.

gold-plated—Any of several processes by which a base metal is covered with gold.

gripper—A needlework clamp that served as a third hand to hold work in progress.

gutta-percha—A resin much like rubber but harder and easily molded, usually dark brown in color.

haribako—A wooden, Japanese sewing box with drawers that had decorative, metal pulls.

hem measure—A flat, metal ruler approximately three to five inches in length, used for marking hems. Some have highly decorative motifs at the top, and most have a sliding sleeve approximately one-half inch long to mark the desired hem length.

hoop—Usually two rings of wood, plastic, or metal, one slightly larger than the other. Fabric is pulled over the first ring, and the second ring is pushed down over the fabric and around the first ring to secure the fabric and offer a more rigid surface to facilitate embroidery. Often the second ring may be tightened by a spring or thumbscrew mechanism.

horn—The horn of any animal, usually indigenous to the place where the tool is made. Used for decorative inlay as well as entire small tools.

hussif—A small sewing kit that is essentially a tube on which the thimble screws as a cap. Dating from the seventeenth century, some are footed to stand upright. Older items are wrought of precious metals, while modern hussifs are made of plastic or base metals and are popular as advertising gimmicks and souvenirs.

(Above) Nanny brooch, brass and goldstone, English, 1880–1910.

Indian—Specifically American and Canadian Indians, whose beaded pincushions are highly collectible and often difficult to distinguish from Victorian, English pieces. The American Indian also produced the sweetgrass tools of the early-twentieth century, which copied European tools in a wonderfully naive and captivating manner.

inlay—The setting of decorative material in the surface or background of an item so that a smooth surface is maintained.

ivorene—A composition of ivory dust with glue and perhaps other ingredients, used to imitate ivory.

ivory—The dental material of a skeletal system, the most common being the tusks of elephants.

Japanware—Japanese lacquerware.

knitting needles—Two or more slender lengths of wire, wood, bone, or other material used to knit garments and household items. They may be found in sets of various gauges and lengths, contained in simple envelopes of fabric or plastic or in handsome boxes that are elaborately decorated. Some have points at both ends; others have a single point with a knob at the other end.

knitting needle gauge—Usually a template with holes equal to the various sizes of knitting needles. A helpful tool in determining needle sizes when the needles are unmarked or from a source with a different sizing system.

knitting needle guards—A single item or a pair of items designed to fit over the ends of the knitting needles to prevent stitches from slipping off when work is not in progress.

knitting sheath—Usually made of wood, the sheath slips into the waistband of a knitter's clothing with one end and with the other end holds a knitting needle securely in place so that the knitter is free to use one hand for putting stitches on the needle. A sheath is usually curved or has a bit of a hook shape at the end that is inserted into the belt or waistband.

knotting shuttle—A tool much like a tatting shuttle in appearance but much larger and with blunt ends. It is used to knot cord for appliqué on fabric.

lace bobbin—A spindle-shaped bobbin used in lacemaking, it is turned so that knobs hold the wound thread near the top of the spindle. The handle of the bobbin usually terminates with string or wire thread with colorful beads which, in sets, assist the lacemaker in the sequence of use.

lace bobbin box—A box specifically designed to hold lace bobbins. Very rare.

lacemaker's box—A workbox fitted with the essential tools for lacemaking, including a lacemaker's pillow, patterns, scissors, pins, bobbins, etc.

lacemaker's pillow—A pillow shaped in the traditional manner, or sometimes cylindrical in shape, upon which the lacemaker pins her patterns and executes her work.

lacquerware—Any article finished with lacquer or varnish, whether as a final finish or as a fixative for decorative work. The finish usually is high gloss but may be sanded to a patina.

lady's companion—A small sewing case, offspring of the etui, which holds tools in an upright position. It holds only sewing and writing tools and is usually simpler in design than the etui or nécessaire.

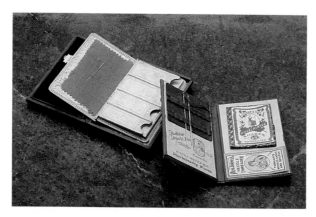

(Above) Needlebooks: 1) Brass, in leather presentation case, Victorian, R. J. Robert's "Unique," English, c. 1870; 2) Artificial leather with gold embossing, holds needles and needle threader, American, c. 1900. Photos show both pieces open (top) and closed (bottom).

lathe—A woodworker's machine on which work is held and turned for shaping. Also, a movable frame on a loom that facilitates the positioning of warp and weft threads.

leather—The skin of an animal, tanned or otherwise treated for use. It is used alone or in combination with other materials, for the covering as well as the lining of needlework boxes and containers.

loom—Any frame or machine upon which fabric is woven. It may be used to weave yards of fine fabric or a simple pot holder.

lucet—A two-pronged fork, sometimes attached to a handle, that is used to make cord. While the lucet may have been used alone, occasionally a small hook or stiletto was used to facilitate removal of loops of thread from the prongs or "horns."

lyre—Another term for a lucet.

mahogany—A reddish yellow hardwood used for a variety of needlework tools, both large and small, including sewing stands, swifts, and small containers.

maple—The hard, close-grained, light wood of the maple tree. There is a variety of maple woods, including bird's eye, curly, and rock, that may be used in tools and containers.

marquetry—The inlay, particularly of different colored woods, to form a design in the surface of a wooden object. Earliest marquetry was done with veneers and later with grain-end mosaics, a process perfected in Tunbridge Wells, England. As Berlin work became popular, patterns were executed in colored woods to form flowers, etc.

Mauchline—A city in Scotland famed for the production of Scottish tartanware.

mitrailleuse—Named for a nineteenth-century machine gun, the mitrailleuse is a needlecase divided into sections, each holding a different size needle. By turning the top on the cylindrical case, a small hole may be positioned over the section that holds the needles of choice.

mother-of-pearl—The white, iridescent nacre that lines the shells of mollusks. Used for inlay, buttons and buckles, and individual tools.

mutton ivory—Any ivory substitute that did not come from an animal.

nail—An old unit of measure approximately two-and-one-quarter inches long derived from the distance between nails or tacks hammered into a measuring stick. The expression "getting down to brass tacks" came from the final measuring of fabric or ribbon once merchants had dickered over the price of ells.

nanny brooch—A brooch, usually of brass, that is like a tube on a pin. Within the tube is a needle and a tiny spool wound with thread. The items are easily retrieved for emergency mending of the garments of a nanny's charges.

nécessaire—A small, fitted, needlework implement container that holds the tools in a vertical position. Personal toiletry items might also be included in the same case. Often covered with leather and gold-tooled. (See lady's companion.)

needle—A sewing instrument, with a point at one end and an eye at the other, used for drawing thread through fabric. Material, size, and sharpness of the implement may be altered to accommodate different sewing needs. (See knitting needles, netting needle.)

needlebook—Leaves of fabric in which needles are kept, bound like a reading book in a variety of covers, often to match other tools in a set.

needlebox—A container in which packets of needles are kept.

needlecase—A hollow tube in which needles are kept. Made of every conceivable material in every possible shape. Some are suspended from chatelaines; others are included in workboxes, etuis, and kits; still others are unique in style and size.

needle packet—Originally, papers folded over a number of loose needles to hold them for ease of sale. Often the packet bore the label of the manufacturer. Later, a folded piece of heavy paper in which needles are held in foil or parchment sheets that are glued to the heavier backing. The later versions were popular advertising giveaways. Modern needle packets are usually bubble or blister packs.

needle threader—A fine-wire loop formed into a point, the ends of which are fastened to a firmer material that may be held between thumb and finger. The wire is passed through the eye of the needle, the thread is passed through the loop, and then the loop is pulled back through the eye, bringing the thread with it.

needlework clamp—Any of a number of devices, that were attached to a stable

(Top) Needlecases: *1)* Sterling silver figural, in the shape of Napoleon, European, 1820–1860; *2)* Ivory, umbrella with bear at top end of handle, Chinese, c. 1850; *3)* Walnut, holds large darners and tapestry needles, probably English, c. 1900; *4)* Vegetable ivory, both ends unscrew, English, 1850–1890. *(Above)* Pincushions: *1)* Chick, sterling with red-velvet cushion, English, c. 1907; *2)* Duck, sterling with green-velvet cushion, English, c. 1907; *3)* Disc, heart-shaped advertisement, American, c. 1940; *4)* Large, cotton, advertisement for "Sylko" thread, English, c. 1930.

(Above) Silver-plated reel stand, unusual because it is of a fine metal, English, possibly 1920.

surface with a bracket and thumbscrew to aid the needleworker. Occasionally found in pairs for winding thread.

netting needle—A long needle split at each end to admit thread into an oval eye. It was used in conjunction with a netting mesh: a smooth, preferably flat implement, almost like a Popsicle® stick, to make netting. The size of the loops of a piece of netting depends upon both tools.

O.N.T.—Found on product from Clark and Co., thread manufacturers, the letters stand for "Our New Thread."

ormolu—A variety of brass made to give the appearance of gold.

oroide—An alloy of copper and zinc or copper and tin, which looks gold in color.

Palais Royale—Pertaining to needlework tools and French workboxes and implements, the most identifiable of which are those made of mother-of-pearl and marked with a tiny, enameled pansy. Because of their fragility, they are very rare.

paper—Used to line some needlework boxes and to decorate the surfaces of tools and containers. For example, later tartanware was covered with a printed plaid rather than being hand-painted.

papier mâché—Used in place of wood, in several layers, to make workboxes. The careful finishing of some boxes is so fine that the box may be mistaken for wood.

patchwork—The sewing together of pieces of fabric, randomly or in a pattern. Pincushions were sometimes made in this manner.

peddler's doll—A doll of six to eight inches in height that is constructed so that her clothing holds sewing implements.

pewter—An alloy having tin as its principle element.

piercer—Another name for a stiletto.

pin—Originally a sharp piece of metal or wood used to hold clothing together, the pin is now a piece of wire with a sharp point at one end and a head at the other. Collectors will find papers of pins and boxes of pins the best way to add to a collection. Black mourning pins in their original box are a find.

pinchbeck—An alloy of copper and zinc made to imitate gold.

pincushion—A receptacle for pins into which the pin is thrust until it is needed. There are disc, ball, figural, and pillow-style pincushions made of every type of material.

plastic—Organic or synthetic material that may be formed into a usable item usually by molding.

poppet—A pincushion within a container that may be closed to save the pins. Designed to be carried in a pocket or purse.

porcelain—A ceramic of high quality, translucent, and hard. Tools, often thimbles, are made more as collector's pieces rather than those of service because of their fragility.

prisoner-of-war work—Items made by prisoners, particularly those of the Napoleonic period, which were bartered for food and other personal needs. Because straw was readily available to prisoners, it was the material most commonly used. Unfortunately, most straw work is attributed to prisoners, which is not the case.

(Above left) Scissors: 1) Fine, figural, for embroidery, sterling with steel blades, in matching sheath, bows fashioned to look like pheasants, French, 1830–1860; 2) Figural, for embroidery, steel, shanks fashioned to resemble a rooster, German, 1890–1920; 3) Chinese, in black, embroidered, silk case, 1890–1930; 4) Single steel "scissors," double blade with spring action from curved shank, origin unknown. (Above right) 1) Sewing bird clamp with two pincushions, American, c. 1853; 2) Metal clamp with swinging, grooved attachment to hold fabric, English or American, early twentieth century.

punch—Another name for a stiletto, but correctly one of a strong-enough point to pierce materials heavier than fabric.

reel—Two discs connected by a shank. One disc (considered the top disc, usually carved or otherwise decorated) may be removed to accommodate a spool of thread. Usually made of bone, ivory, or mother-of-pearl, matched sets are rare but are sometimes found in fitted workboxes.

reel stand—Another name for a spool stand.

reverse glass painting—Decorative painting on the back or inside of an item of glass. Eventually replaced by paper prints, pieces of a commemorative nature were often affixed to the top of flat items, such as disc pincushions and needlebooks.

ribbon threader—A flat tool with a slit at one end and a large, round eye at the other, used for pulling ribbon or cord through eyelet, casings, and insertion. (See bodkin.)

rosewood—Wood of various reddish colors streaked with black. Highly valued, it comes from several tropical and subtropical trees.

sandalwood—A close-grained, fragrant, yellowish wood that comes from a parasitic tree in the Indo-Malaysian area.

satinwood—A yellow- or orange-colored wood from trees akin to the mahogany family.

scissors—A cutting instrument made of two blades, each attached by a shank to a bow, or ring, that is large enough to accommodate a finger. Specialty scissors are made to cut buttonholes or to pink raw edges of fabric. Small scissors, under six inches, are called scissors; large scissors are called shears. Very old scissors may be made of a single strip of metal, with blades honed at either end and bent in the middle to serve as a spring.

scissors sharpener—A metal plate with a hole divided by a sharpening rod, which would accommodate the two blades of a pair of scissors. The blades are drawn through the hole against the rod to sharpen them.

scissors sheath—A cover for the blades, and sometimes the shanks, of a pair of scissors. Intended to protect the points. Sheaths are often suspended from chatelaines to hold scissors; others are made for individual pairs of scissors.

(Top) Tatting shuttles: *1) Brass, marked "Justrite," American, c. 1930; 2) Mother-of-pearl with abalone inset, English, 1850–1870.* *(Above left)* Silkwinders: *1) Mother-of-pearl, from French workbox, c. 1850; 2) Mother-of-pearl, Chinese for European market, c. 1850.* *(Above right)* Sterling silver spool knave, spring-style pin, English, c. 1870.

Scottish souvenir ware—Nineteenth-century sewing tools from Scotland, which included tartanware, fernware, and transferware.

sewing bird—A sewing clamp that was made in the figure of a bird whose beak opened to hold fabric. Clamps with other animals are erroneously called sewing birds; they should be called by their particular names.

sewing case—Usually a flat case fitted to hold sewing tools, much like a modern watch box. Etuis, nécessaires, and lady's companions may also be called sewing cases.

sewing kits—Small, usually hand-sized kits that contain tools and thread. The hussif is a sewing kit. Advertising kits may be as small as a matchbook, holding needle, thread, and a button or two.

shagreen—Untanned leather, sometimes attributed to sharkskin.

shell work—Decorative work with the shells of mollusks. Whole shells may be fitted as pincushions or with findings to convert a bivalve into a box.

shepherd's hook—Another name for a crochet hook.

shuttle—A tool upon which thread or yarn is wound and from which it is drawn

as work progresses, as with a tatting or knotting shuttle. Early sewing machine bobbins are sometimes called shuttles.

silk—The fine thread drawn from the cocoon of the silk worm. As a thread, it was used for embroidery. As a fabric, it lines or covers needlework-tool containers.

silkwinder—Usually a flat, notched or grooved tool upon which silk or other thread is wound. The predecessor of the spool.

silver—A precious metal of gray color. Highly malleable, it is often alloyed to add strength. Sterling silver, which should be marked as such, is .925 fine.

silver filigree—The application of very fine silver wire over a silver or other base to decorate the surface.

silver plate—Any means by which another material is covered by a layer of silver.

Solingen—A German city known for superior steel production and as the source of fine scissors to this day.

spinning wheel—A hand- or foot-driven wheel by which thread or yarn is spun from raw material.

spool—A thread container upon which thread is wound directly and drawn off as needed for sewing. Shaped like a wide

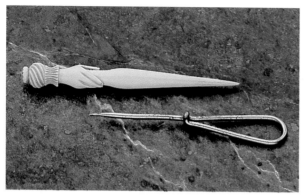

(Above left) Stilettos: **1)** Ivory, finial is finely carved hand, Chinese for export, c. 1820; **2)** Bent steel, handle and point are all of one piece, origin unknown. (Above right) Assorted thimbles: **1)** Nickel-silver, American, c. 1900; **2)** Silver, American, c. 1900; **3)** Gold, American, c. 1920; **4)** Brass, English, 1880–1930; **5)** Aluminum, child's, American, c. 1940; **6)** Steel, tailor's, English, c. 1900; **7)** Enamel on sterling silver, German, early twentieth century; **8)** Hand-painted porcelain, American, c. 1940; **9)** Plastic thimble, American advertisement, c. 1950.

dowel that broadens at the ends to prevent the thread from slipping off. Usually of turned wood or molded plastic. Early spools that are of ivory or bone may be found.

spool knave—Attached at the waist with a hook or a pin, the spool knave consists of a chain that holds, in a horseshoe or C-shaped receptacle, a bar on which a spool may be held. Its purpose is to allow thread to be pulled smoothly while working. It is particularly handy when doing such surface embroidery as tambouring.

spool stand—A stand from which multiple dowels or wires extend vertically to hold multiple spools.

(Above) Tape measures: **1)** Celluloid basket of flowers, with spring action, German, 1900–1930; **2)** Brass shoe, with spring action, inscribed "Three feet in one shoe," American, 1900–1920.

Stanhope—A tiny, glass rod that served as a lens through which scenes and portraits could be seen when held close to the eye. Often found atop needlecases during the nineteenth century.

steel—Iron that has been alloyed with carbon to form a strong, malleable gray metal. Used particularly for the blades of scissors and stilettos and for needles and pins.

stiletto—A sharp, pointed, rounded blade, usually attached to a handle, that is used to "worry" holes in cloth or to pierce heavy materials. Some stilettos made of one piece of bone, mother-of-pearl, or ivory were not suitable for piercing anything but fabric. Also called piercers. Some may have an eye at the end so that they may double as bodkins.

stone—In reference to needlework tools, precious stones were often used to decorate items of precious metal. Roman thimbles that were carved of stone have been found.

straw work—The decorative work done with bits of straw on needlework tools and their containers, usually in a mosaic pattern.

sumac—A tree or shrub that serves as a source of natural varnish.

sweetgrass—Used by Native Americans during the Victorian era to weave into imitations of needlework tools.

swift—A reel that has arms that expand to accommodate large skeins of thread or yarn. Knitters often use swifts to hold wool while wrapping it into balls. Some may be mounted on clamps; others are freestanding.

tambour—A frame, much like a drum, for surface embroidery, particularly tambouring, which is constructed of two U-shaped pieces of wood that are held together in the center, where they are crossed by screws or brads and by a hoop at their ends. Fabric stretched over the hoop is secured by a second hoop or a belt for a tight surface.

tambour hook—A hook with a sharp point, which can pierce fabric, on the external curve. Once the hook is passed through the fabric, it can draw up a loop. A series of loops then form a chain on the fabric's surface.

tape measure—A ribbon upon which units of linear measure are marked to assist in the determination of a length of thread or fabric, the proportions of a garment, etc. Containers upon which the tape may be wound are made of all possible materials. Some are manually wound; others are retracted by a spring mechanism.

tartanware—Items upon which a tartan design was hand painted or varnished in place. While not yet rare, tools and containers of this type are costly.

tatting shuttle—Two elliptical plates with pointed ends, which are held together by a centerpiece that acts as a bobbin for thread of various weights. The points of the plates are curved toward each other so that they almost touch. Occasionally a hook is wrought on one of the points. By making a series of knots and loops with the shuttle, an airy fabric or trim may be constructed.

tatting shuttle case—A case for holding a tatting shuttle. Very rare.

thimble—Any small device fitted over the end of the finger to protect it from being pricked by a needle or pin. There are specialty thimbles for tailors and quilters: patented thimbles that grip needles or have blades attached with which to cut thread. Of all needlework tools, there are more thimbles made than anything else except needles. Ornamental thimbles (those impractical for sewing) have been manufactured in great quantities as commemorative, souvenir, and advertising ploys. (See finger guard.)

thimble case—A container for a thimble, which may hang from a chatelaine, fit in a workbox, or be manufactured separately for individual purchase. Made of most durable materials, most have a snap, screw, or friction closure.

thimble stand—An ornamental stand that holds a thimble when not in use. It is designed to sit on a table or shelf and has no cover.

thread—Artificial or natural fibers spun or twisted into fine lengths for sewing of all types.

thread container—A box that may hold a single spool or reel, or several such items. Matched or graduated sets of spools often come in larger containers while a single container might be suspended from a chatelaine.

thread winder—(See cotton barrel, spool, bobbins, and silkwinder.)

tin—A malleable, gray-white metal used for containers of quotidian items such as pins or tiny commemorative or advertising kits.

tortoiseshell—The horny substance from a tortoise, particularly the hawksbill tortoise, used for covering large surfaces and for ornamental work. Plastics have been mottled to imitate the shell, but they do not hold the high gloss that the genuine shell holds.

tracing wheel—A notched wheel attached by a shank to a handle. Rolled over pattern paper around a template or other pattern, it duplicated or created a new pattern.

transferware—Items upon which prints of scenic and famous places are transferred to the surface(s) of wooden tools and tool containers.

Tunbridgeware—Manufactured in Tunbridge Wells, these wares were of very high-quality mosaic work. End-grain

mosaic work, fine veneers, and exceptional marquetry identify Tunbridgeware.

vegetable ivory—Originally a term used to identify the shell of the corozo nut, it is often ascribed to the coquilla seed.

velvet—Used both for the lining and the covering of needlework boxes and for the covering of pincushions and emeries, it is a napped fabric with various depths of pile. It is usually made of cotton or silk.

waxer—Any style of tool that enables the needleworker to draw thread across a cake of white wax or beeswax in **order** to add strength to the thread. Most often found in disc-styled tools.

wicker—Originally the pliant twigs of the willow tree, the term now applies to most of the natural materials from which a basket may be woven. Chinese sewing baskets decorated with glass rings, beads, coins, and tassels were popular during the early twentieth century and are often called wicker sewing baskets.

(Above) Glove darner, painted wood, American, c. 1920.
(Left) Lady's companion, cut-steel tools in lacquered wood box, European, c. 1840.

winding clamps—A pair of needlework clamps around which skeins of thread are wound in preparation for division into smaller amounts.

wire—Of precious metals, wire was couched on the surface of fabric for clothing and ornamental room hangings. Of baser metals, it was used for beadwork.

workbox—A term used for a box that served to contain tools peculiar to a trade or profession. Used among needlewomen as a term for what is more specifically called a fitted needlework box.

workstand—A term used for a sewing stand that opens by means of a lid. Not only will it hold tools, but there is also room for the needlewoman's work.

EDITOR'S NOTE
Some of the tools illustrating this article are from private collections. Others are from Anne Powell, Ltd. Turn to page 142 for catalog ordering information.

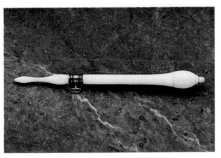

(Above left) Lucet, ivory, European, 1790–1810.
(Above right) Knotting shuttle, tortoise, c. 1800.
(Left) Tambour hook, ivory, probably French, c. 1800.

SOURCES FOR SUPPLIES

Page 6—Wool from The Attic Antiques, 5620 Cahaba Valley Road (Highway 119), Birmingham, AL 35242; 1878 marriage license, antique photos, nineteenth-century Bible, and French carved box from Hanna Antiques, Inc., 2424 Seventh Avenue South, Birmingham, AL 35233; 1880 newspaper from Historic Newspaper Archives, Inc., 1582 Hart Street, Rahway, NJ 07065; brass looking glass from Maralyn Wilson Gallery, 2010 Cahaba Road, Birmingham, AL 35223.

Frances Lawson Sampler

Page 8—Tassel from Scalamandré, 950 Third Avenue, New York, NY 10022; remaining props from The Attic Antiques.

Elizabeth Burcham Sampler

Page 14—Books from Books! by George at Hanna Antiques, Inc.; remaining props from Hanna Antiques, Inc.

Dorothy Preston Sampler

Page 20—40-count linen available from Em-Li's, 1004 West Cumberland Street, Dunn, NC 28334, (910)892-3083.

Frances Jewkes Sampler

Page 34—Nineteenth-century Bible and French carved box from Hanna Antiques, Inc.

Eighteenth-Century Floral

Page 45—Chair and bed from Andrea's Heirlooms & Gifts at Hanna Antiques, Inc.; linen thread available from Textile Reproductions. [For a catalog of the company's offerings, send $4.00 to Textile Reproductions, Post Office Box 48, Department SAN 94, West Chesterfield, MA 01084, (413)296-4437. Free, linen-thread sample card available with catalog request.].

Rose Bouquet

Page 48—Oval box available from Anne Brinkley Designs, 761 Palmer Avenue, Holmdel, NJ 07733 (908)787-2011; pillows from Andrea's Heirlooms & Gifts at Hanna Antiques, Inc.; jewelry, perfume bottle, and hand brush from Hanna Antiques, Inc.

Needlework Casket

Page 52—Seventeenth-century ladies' travel casket available from Creative Furnishings, 12357 Saraglen Drive, Saratoga, CA 95070, (408)996-7745; chest, photo, and textiles from Andrea's Heirlooms & Gifts at Hanna Antiques, Inc.

Greek-Key Sampler

Page 75—Pipe, tea box, cigarette dispenser, jewelry box, English toothpick holder, and Irish inlaid sideboard from Hanna Antiques, Inc.; brass looking glass from Maralyn Wilson Gallery.

From the Heart Sampler

Page 79—Table and trims from Andrea's Heirlooms & Gifts at Hanna Antiques, Inc.

Harvest Sampler

Page 82—Candle from Maralyn Wilson Gallery; candle holder and bowl from Richard Tubb, Dr. Pepper Building, 2829 Second Avenue South, Birmingham, AL 35233.

Peace Sampler

Page 88—Shelf and pincushion from The Attic Antiques; horn from Hanna Antiques, Inc.; tassel from Scalamandré.

Embroidered Purse

Page 94—Table from Andrea's Heirlooms & Gifts at Hanna Antiques, Inc.; earrings from Richard Tubb.

Heart Sampler

Page 99—Pitcher, glass, and linens from The Attic Antiques.

Hearts and Flowers Accessories

Page 108—Table from Andrea's Heirlooms & Gifts at Hanna Antiques, Inc.; silk ribbon available from C. A.'s Eclectic Collection, 3617 Harvard Avenue, Dallas, TX 75205-3225, FAX (214)528-1685; workbox available from Home Arts, 1-800-484-9923, PIN # 2787.

Trio of Hearts

Page 123—Knob, key, and decoupage box from Hanna Antiques, Inc.

Shaker-Box Samplers

Page 127—Shaker boxes available from Sudberry House, Inc. [For a catalog of the company's offerings, send $2.50 to Sudberry House, Inc., Box 895, Old Lyme, CT 06371, (203)739-6951.].

A Glossary for Collectors of Needlework Tools

Page 132—Selected antique needlework tools from Anne Powell, Ltd. [For a catalog of the company's offerings, send $5.00 to Anne Powell, Ltd., Post Office Box 3060, Stuart, FL 34995, (407) 287-3007]; marble from Yaffa Stone Corporation, 2836 Mary Taylor Road, Birmingham, AL 35210.

Items not included in "Sources for Supplies" are either commonly available, antiques, or from private collections. Antiques included in "Sources for Supplies" were available from the merchants listed at the time photography was completed. Availability may vary depending on each merchant's sales since that time.

Artists and Artisans

Stitches in Time

Dorothy Preston Sampler, page 20, reproduced by Catherine G. Scott, stitched by Kayla Connors and Carol Norris

Elizabeth Burcham Sampler, page 14, reproduced by Marie Barber, stitched by Betti Abrecht

Frances Jewkes Sampler, page 34, reproduced and stitched by Catherine G. Scott

Frances Lawson Sampler, page 8, reproduced by Marie Barber, stitched by Catherine G. Scott

Treasures for Tomorrow

Eighteenth-Century Floral, page 45, designed by Anne Wilson Stanton, stitched by Margaret Taylor

From the Heart Sampler, page 79, designed and stitched by Dawn Lewis, The Needle's Work

Greek-Key Sampler, page 75, designed and stitched by Anna I. Jackson

Harvest Sampler, page 82, designed by Teresa Wentzler

Marriage Sampler, page 68, designed by Angela Pullen, stitched by Judy Thaxton

Needlework Casket, page 52, designed by Phyllis Hoffman, stitched by Stephanie Burrows, Bettye Dwyer, Carol Norris, April Taylor, and Judy Thaxton

Peace Sampler, page 88, designed by Cathy Livingston, stitched by Rebecca Langston

Rose Bouquet, page 48, designed by Angela Pullen, stitched by Angela Pullen and Margaret Taylor

Elegance in White

Embroidered Purse, page 94, reproduced by Claudia B. Wood, stitched by Carol Norris

Heart Sampler, page 99, designed by Teresa Wentzler, stitched by Carol Norris

Diminutive Works

Christmas Sampler, page 105, designed by Phyllis Hoffman, stitched by Bettye Dwyer and April Taylor

Hearts and Flowers Accessories, page 108, designed and stitched by C. A. Wells

Shaker-Box Samplers, page 127, designed by Angela Pullen, stitched by Catherine G. Scott and Tonda Zimmerman

Trio of Hearts, page 123, designed and stitched by Anne Wilson Stanton

Computer Charting

Lea Burks, Rebecca Mitchell

Custom Finishing

Tonda Williams, Claudia B. Wood

Acknowledgements

The editors wish to gratefully acknowledge the generosity of the following companies and individuals who have provided materials for the production of the models and the props and locations used for photographing them.

AK Designs
Alice and Julian Dunklin
Anne Brinkley Designs
The Attic Antiques
The Caron Collection
Charles Craft, Inc.
The DMC Corporation
Francis Land House
Gay Bowles Sales
Hanna Antiques, Inc.
Home Arts

J. & P. Coats/Anchor®
Kreinik Manufacturing
Maralyn Wilson Gallery
Norden Crafts
Pat & Pam Designs
Textile Reproductions
Wichelt Imports, Inc.
Yaffa Stone Corporation
YLI Corporation
Zweigart®

Index

Numbers in **bold** type indicate color-photo pages. All other numbers refer to pages for charts, color codes, patterns, and instructions.